U.S. Department of Justice
Office of Justice Programs
National Institute of Justice

National Institute of Justice

Law Enforcement and Corrections Standards and Testing Program

Guide for the Selection of Personal Protective Equipment for Emergency First Responders (Respiratory Protection)

NIJ Guide 102–00

Volume IIa
November 2002

U.S. Department of Justice
Office of Justice Programs
810 Seventh Street N.W.
Washington, DC 20531

John Ashcroft
Attorney General

Deborah J. Daniels
Assistant Attorney General

Sarah V. Hart
Director, National Institute of Justice

For grant and funding information, contact:
Department of Justice Response Center
800–421–6770

Office of Justice Programs
World Wide Web Site
http://www.ojp.usdoj.gov

National Institute of Justice
World Wide Web Site
http://www.ojp.usdoj.gov/nij

U.S. Department of Justice
Office of Justice Programs
National Institute of Justice

Guide for the Selection of Personal Protective Equipment for Emergency First Responders (Respiratory Protection)

NIJ Guide 102–00, Volume IIa

Dr. Alim A. Fatah[1]
John A. Barrett[2]
Richard D. Arcilesi, Jr.[2]
Charlotte H. Lattin[2]
Charles G. Janney[2]
Edward A. Blackman[2]

Coordination by:
Office of Law Enforcement Standards
National Institute of Standards and Technology
Gaithersburg, MD 20899–8102

Prepared for:
National Institute of Justice
Office of Science and Technology
Washington, DC 20531

November 2002

This document was prepared under CBIAC contract number SPO–900–94–D–0002 and Interagency Agreement M92361 between NIST and the Department of Defense Technical Information Center (DTIC).

NCJ 191519

---

[1] National Institute of Standards and Technology, Office of Law Enforcement Standards.
[2] Battelle Memorial Institute.

National Institute of Justice

Sarah V. Hart
Director

This guide was prepared for the National Institute of Justice, U.S. Department of Justice, by the Office of Law Enforcement Standards of the National Institute of Standards and Technology under Interagency Agreement 94–IJ–R–004, Project No. 99–060–CBW. It was also prepared under CBIAC contract No. SPO–900–94–D–0002 and Interagency Agreement M92361 between NIST and the Department of Defense Technical Information Center (DTIC).

The authors wish to thank Ms. Kathleen Higgins of the National Institute of Standards and Technology, Mr. Bill Haskell of SBCCOM, Ms. Priscilla S. Golden of General Physics, LTC Don Buley of the Joint Program Office of Biological Defense, Ms. Nicole Trudel of Camber Corporation, Dr. Stephen Morse of Centers for Disease Control, and Mr. Todd Brethauer of the Technical Support Working Group for their significant contributions to this effort. We would also like to acknowledge the Interagency Board for Equipment Standardization and Interoperability, which consists of Government and first responder representatives.

FOREWORD

NIJ is the research, development, and evaluation agency of the U.S. Department of Justice and is solely dedicated to researching crime control and justice issues. NIJ provides objective, independent, nonpartisan, evidence-based knowledge and tools to meet the challenges of crime and justice, particularly at the State and local levels.

The NIJ Director is appointed by the President and confirmed by the Senate. The Director establishes the Institute's objectives and is guided by the priorities of the Office of Justice Programs, the U.S. Department of Justice, and the needs of the field. The Institute actively solicits the views of criminal justice and other professionals and researchers to inform its search for the knowledge and tools to guide policy and practice.

In partnership with others, NIJ's mission is to prevent and reduce crime, improve law enforcement and the administration of justice, and promote public safety. By applying the disciplines of the social and physical sciences, NIJ:

- Researches the nature and impact of crime and delinquency.
- Develops applied technologies, standards, and tools for criminal justice practitioners.
- Evaluates existing programs and responses to crime.
- Tests innovative concepts and program models in the field.
- Assists policymakers, program partners, and justice agencies.
- Disseminates knowledge to many audiences.

As part of its standard development activities, NIJ serves as the executive agent for the Interagency Board for Equipment Standardization and Interoperability (IAB). The IAB has developed a set of priorities for standards for equipment to be used by first responders to critical incidents, including terrorist incidents relating to chemical, biological, nuclear, radiological, and explosive weapons. In particular, the development of chemical and biological defense equipment guides for the emergency first responder community is a high priority of NIJ.

The Office of Law Enforcement Standards (OLES) of the National Institute of Standards and Technology (NIST) furnishes technical support to NIJ in the development of standards. OLES subjects existing equipment to laboratory testing and evaluation and conducts research leading to the development of national standards, user guides, and technical reports.

This document covers research conducted by OLES under the sponsorship of NIJ. Other NIJ documents developed by OLES cover protective clothing and equipment, communications systems, emergency equipment, investigative aids, security systems, vehicles, weapons, analytical techniques, and standard reference materials used by the forensic community.

Technical comments and suggestions concerning this guide are invited from all interested parties. They may be addressed to the Office of Law Enforcement Standards, National Institute of Standards and Technology, 100 Bureau Drive, Stop 8102, Gaithersburg, MD 20899–8102.

Sarah V. Hart, Director
National Institute of Justice

CONTENTS

FOREWORD iii

COMMONLY USED SYMBOLS AND ABBREVIATIONS vi

ABOUT THIS GUIDE ix

1. INTRODUCTION 1

2. IDENTIFICATION OF PERSONAL PROTECTION EQUIPMENT 3

    2.1 Identification of New Equipment 3

    2.2 Vendor Contact 3

3. DATA FIELDS 5

    3.1 General Category 5

    3.2 Operational Parameters Category 7

    3.3 Physical Parameters Category 8

    3.4 Logistical Parameters Category 9

    3.5 Special Requirements Category 11

APPENDIX A—REFERENCES A–1

APPENDIX B—INDEX BY RESPIRATORY PROTECTIVE EQUIPMENT
    IDENTIFICATION NUMBER B–1

APPENDIX C—INDEX BY RESPIRATORY PROTECTIVE EQUIPMENT NAME C–1

APPENDIX D—INDEX BY RESPIRATORY PROTECTIVE EQUIPMENT
    MANUFACTURER D–1

APPENDIX E—RESPIRATORY PROTECTIVE EQUIPMENT DATA SHEETS E–1

COMMONLY USED SYMBOLS AND ABBREVIATIONS

A	ampere	H	hour	oz.	ounce
ac	alternating current	Hf	high frequency	No.	number
AM	amplitude modulation	Hz	hertz	o.d.	outside diameter
cd	candela	i.d.	inside diameter	Ω	ohm
cm	centimeter	In	inch	p.	page
CP	chemically pure	IR	infrared	Pa	pascal
c/s	cycle per second	J	joule	pe	probable error
d	day	L	lambert	pp.	pages
dB	decibel	L	liter	ppm	parts per million
dc	direct current	Lb	pound	qt	quart
°C	degree Celsius	Lbf	pound-force	rad	radian
°F	degree Fahrenheit	lbf·in	pound-force inch	rf	radio frequency
dia	diameter	Lm	lumen	rh	relative humidity
emf	electromotive force	Ln	logarithm (base e)	s	second
eq	equation	Log	logarithm (base 10)	SD	standard deviation
F	farad	M	molar	sec.	Section
fc	footcandle	M	meter	SWR	standing wave ratio
fig.	Figure	μ	micron	uhf	ultrahigh frequency
FM	frequency modulation	Min	minute	UV	ultraviolet
ft	foot	M m	millimeter	V	volt
ft/s	foot per second	Mph	miles per hour	vhf	very high frequency
g	acceleration	m/s	meter per second	W	watt
g	gram	M o	month	λ	wavelength
gal	gallon	N	newton	wk	week
gr	grain	N·m	newton meter	wt	weight
H	henry	Nm	nanometer	yr	year

area=unit^2 (e.g., ft^2, in^2, etc.); volume=unit^3 (e.g., ft^3, m^3, etc.)

ACRONYMS SPECIFIC TO THIS DOCUMENT

ASTM	American Society for Testing and Materials	NFPA	National Fire Protection Association
BW	Biological Warfare	NIJ	National Institute of Justice
CB	Chemical and Biological	NIOSH	National Institute for Occupational Safety and Health
CBW	Chemical Biological Warfare	NIST	National Institute of Standards and Technology
CPU	Collective Protective Undergarment	NATO	North Atlantic Treaty Organization
CW	Chemical Warfare	NBC	Nuclear, Biological, and Chemical
DOD	Department of Defense	OSHA	Occupational Safety and Health Administration
DPG	Dugway Proving Grounds	PAPR	Powered Air Purifying Respirator
DRES	Defense Research Establishment Suffield	PF	Protection Factor
ECBE	Edgewood Chemical Biological Center, Aberdeen Proving Ground, MD	POL	Petroleum, Oils, and Lubricants
EOD	Explosive Ordnance Disposal	PPE	Personal Protection Equipment
EPA	Environmental Protection Agency	PPV	Positive Pressure Ventilation
ERDEC	U.S. Army Edgewood Research, Development and Engineering Center	PVC	Polyvinyl chloride
FBI	Federal Bureau of Investigation	SBCCOM	U.S. Army Soldier and Biological Chemical Command
FR	Fire Resistant	SCBA	Self-Contained Breathing Apparatus
HAZMAT	Hazardous Materials	SCFM	Standard Cubic Feet per Minute
IDLH	Immediately Dangerous to Life and Health	TAP	Toxicological Agent Protective
IAB	Interagency Board	TICs	Toxic Industrial Chemicals
IDLH	Immediately Dangerous to Life and Health	TIMs	Toxic Industrial Materials
IAB	Interagency Board	TOP	Test Operating Procedure
ITAR	International Traffic and Arms Regulations	TSWG	Technical Support Working Group

PREFIXES (See ASTM E380)

d	deci (10^{-1})	da	deka (10)
c	centi (10^{-2})	h	hecto (10^2)
m	milli (10^{-3})	k	kilo (10^3)
μ	micro (10^{-6})	M	mega (10^6)
n	nano (10^{-9})	G	giga (10^9)
p	pico (10^{-12})	T	tera (10^{12})

COMMON CONVERSIONS

0.30480 m = 1 ft	4.448222 N = 1 lbf
25.4 mm = 1 in	1.355818 J = 1 ft·lbf
0.4535924 kg = 1 lb	0.1129848 N m = 1 lbf·in
0.06479891g = 1gr	14.59390 N/m = 1 lbf/ft
0.9463529 L = 1 qt	6894.757 Pa = 1 lbf/in^2
3600000 J = 1 kW·hr	1.609344 km/h = 1 mph
psi = mm of Hg x (1.9339 x 10^{-2})	
mm of Hg = psi x 51.71	

Temperature: $T_C = (T_F - 32) \times 5/9$ Temperature: $T_F = (T_C \times 9/5) + 32$

ABOUT THIS GUIDE

The National Institute of Justice is the focal point for providing support to State and local law enforcement agencies in the development of counterterrorism technology and standards, including technology needs for chemical and biological defense. In recognizing the needs of State and local emergency first responders, the Office of Law Enforcement Standards (OLES) at the National Institute of Standards and Technology (NIST), supported by the National Institute of Justice (NIJ), the Technical Support Working Group (TSWG), the U.S. Army Soldier and Biological Chemical Command, and the Interagency Board for Equipment Standardization and Interoperability (IAB), is developing chemical and biological defense equipment guides. The guides will focus on chemical and biological equipment in areas of detection, personal protection, decontamination, and communication. This document focuses specifically on assisting the emergency first responder community in the evaluation and purchase of personal protective equipment.

The long range plans are to: (1) subject existing personal protective equipment to laboratory testing and evaluation against a specified protocol, and (2) conduct research leading to the development of multiple series of documents, including national standards, user guides, and technical reports. It is anticipated that the testing, evaluation, and research processes will take several years to complete; therefore, the National Institute of Justice has developed this initial guide for the emergency first responder community in order to facilitate their evaluation and purchase of personal protective equipment.

In conjunction with this program, additional guides, as well as other documents, are being issued in the areas of chemical agent and toxic industrial material detection equipment, biological agent detection equipment, decontamination equipment, and communication equipment.

This Volume, IIa, of the *Guide for the Selection of Personal Protective Equipment for Emergency First Responders*, which focuses particularly on respiratory protection. It contains the information data sheets that were used to support the personal protective equipment evaluation detailed in Volume I. The compilation of data in Volume IIa is the result of the merger of several data acquisition methods used independently by NIST and TSWG.

The information contained in this guide has been obtained through literature searches and market surveys. The vendors were contacted multiple times during the preparation of this guide to ensure data accuracy. In addition, the information is supplemented with test data obtained from other sources (e.g., Department of Defense), if available. It should also be noted that the purpose of this guide is not to provide recommendations but rather to serve as a means to provide information to the reader to compare and contrast commercially available personal protective equipment. *Reference herein to any specific commercial products, processes, or services by trade name, trademark, manufacturer, or otherwise does not necessarily constitute or imply its endorsement, recommendation, or favoring by the United States Government. The information and statements contained in this guide shall not be used for the purposes of advertising, nor to imply the endorsement or recommendation of the United States Government.*

With respect to information provided in this guide, neither the United States Government nor any of its employees make any warranty, expressed or implied, including but not limited to the warranties of merchantability and fitness for a particular purpose. Further, neither the United States Government nor any of its employees assume any legal liability or responsibility for the accuracy, completeness, or usefulness of any information, apparatus, product, or process disclosed.

Technical comments, suggestions, and product updates are encouraged from interested parties. They may be addressed to the Office of Law Enforcement Standards, National Institute of Standards and Technology, 100 Bureau Drive, Stop 8102, Gaithersburg, MD 20899–8102. It is anticipated that this guide will be updated periodically.

Questions relating to the specific devices included in this document should be addressed directly to the proponent agencies or the equipment manufacturers. Contact information for each equipment item included in this guide can be found in this volume (Vol. IIa).

GUIDE FOR THE SELECTION OF PERSONAL PROTECTIVE EQUIPMENT FOR EMERGENCY FIRST RESPONDERS (RESPIRATORY PROTECTION)

This guide includes information intended to be useful to the emergency first responder community in the selection of personal protective equipment (PPE) that includes chemical and biological protective clothing and respiratory equipment for different applications. This Volume, IIa, of the *Guide for the Selection of Personal Protective Equipment for Emergency First Responders*, includes details on the 69 respiratory protective items referenced in Volume I.

1. INTRODUCTION

The *Guide for the Selection of Personal Protective Equipment for Emergency First Responders* includes information intended to be useful to the emergency first responder community in the selection of PPE. Due to the large number of personal protective equipment items identified for the guide, the guide is separated into four volumes. Volume I serves as the selection tool for all PPE items while Volume IIa serves as a repository for the respiratory PPE data sheets; Volume IIb serves as a repository for the percutaneous (garments) PPE data sheets; and Volume IIc serves as a repository for the percutaneous (apparel other than garments) PPE data sheets.

2. IDENTIFICATION OF PERSONAL PROTECTION EQUIPMENT

An extensive market survey was conducted to identify commercially available personal protective equipment. This market survey encompassed the assessment of past market surveys, identification of new equipment, and interaction with numerous equipment vendors.

2.1 Identification of New Equipment

A variety of sources were utilized to identify commercially available personal protective equipment, including a Commerce Business Daily (CBD) Announcement, literature searches, database searches, Internet searches, technical conferences, and technical contacts. These sources resulted in the identification of 69 respiratory protective equipment items.

2.2 Vendor Contact

Vendors were contacted two separate times in order to obtain additional product information, as well as to finalize their specific equipment data for inclusion in the guide. An initial contact occurred in the Fall of 1999, at the Ninth International Society for Respiratory Protection (ISRP) Conference held in Pittsburgh, Pennsylvania, where the manufacturers and vendors supplied detailed information about their products.

The second contact was made during March 2001. Each vendor again received a facsimile or an electronic mail message that contained the data sheets for their specific equipment item(s), the selection factors that were developed to assist with the selection and purchase of the most appropriate equipment, and the results of the evaluation of the respiratory protective equipment against the selection factors. The vendors were asked to review the data sheets and tables for completeness and accuracy of the incorporated data.

3. DATA FIELDS

Appendix E serves as a compendium of commercially available personal protective equipment. Each of the 69 identified respiratory protection equipment items is detailed within appendix E. Forty-nine data fields, as defined in this section, were used for providing information relating to the personal protective equipment. It is important to note that these data fields were developed using input from the emergency responder community.

The data fields are organized into the following five categories:

- General.
- Operational Parameters.
- Physical Parameters.
- Logistical.
- Special Requirements.

The remainder of this section defines each of the 49 data fields by category.

3.1 General Category

The General category includes the following data fields:

1. Name.
2. ID #.
3. Technology.
4. Stock Number.
5. Protection Type.
6. Equipment Category.
7. Availability.
8. Current User.
9. Manufacturer.
10. Manufacturer Type.
11. Developer.
12. Source.
13. Certification.

Each of these data fields is defined in more detail in the remainder of this section.

3.1.1 Name

The Name data field is used to identify the name of the equipment.

3.1.2 ID

The ID # data field is for identification purposes only.

3.1.3 Technology

The Technology data field identifies the processes used to protect the wearer from chemical (CW agents and TIMs), biological agents, and nuclear particulates. Respiratory protection is supplied by physical separation of the agent from the incoming air (i.e., adsorption, condensation), reactive separation (i.e., catalytic oxidation, biofiltration, reactive membranes), or particle separation (i.e., scrubbers, electrostatic precipitation).

3.1.4 Stock Number

The Stock Number data field includes the stock identification or national stock number, if the item has one.

3.1.5 Protection Type

The Protection Type data field identifies whether the equipment provides percutaneous (skin) and/or respiratory protection.

3.1.6 Equipment Category

The Equipment Category data field identifies if the equipment is SCBA, PAPR, tethered air, canister, etc.

3.1.7 Availability

The Availability data field refers to how readily available a piece of equipment is (e.g., how long it takes to receive equipment upon purchasing) or availability status of the equipment (e.g., commercial availability).

3.1.8 Current User

The Current User data field is used to identify organizations that are currently using the piece of equipment.

3.1.9 Manufacturer

The Manufacturer data field indentifies the company that manufactured the piece of equipment (to include the name, address, telephone number, and point-of-contact).

3.1.10 Manufacturer Type

The Manufacturer Type data field indicates whether the manufacturer is domestic or foreign.

3.1.11 Developer

The Developer data field identifies the organization that developed the item. This may be relevant when the developer is the government and the responsible technical agency may need to be identified.

3.1.12 Source

The Source data field indicates where the equipment information was obtained. Potential sources include past market surveys and Internet web sites.

3.1.13 Certification

The Certification data field identifies the agency certifying the system for use (i.e., OSHA, NIOSH, NFPA, etc.), if any.

3.2 Operational Parameters Category

The Operational Parameters category includes the following five data fields:

1. Chemical Warfare (CW) Agents Protection.
2. Biological Warfare (BW) Agents Protection.
3. Toxic Industrial Material (TIMs) Protection.
4. Duration of Protection.
5. Recommended Use(s).

Each of these data fields is defined in more detail in the remainder of this section.

3.2.1 Chemical Warfare (CW) Agents Protection

The Chemical Warfare Agents Protection data field indicates the type of chemical warfare (CW) agent. The most common types of classic CW agents are the nerve and blister agents. Nerve agents include GA (Tabun), GB (Sarin), GD (Soman), GF, and VX. Blister agents include H and HD (Sulfur Mustards), HN (Nitrogen Mustard), and L (Lewisite).

3.2.2 Biological Warfare (BW) Agents Protection

The Biological Warfare (BW) Agents Protection data field indicates the type of biological warfare (BW) agent. Classical BW agents include bacteria (Anthrax), rickettsia (Typhus), toxins (Botulinum Toxin), and viruses (Q Fever).

3.2.3 Toxic Industrial Materials (TIMs) Protection

The Toxic Industrial Materials (TIMs) Protection data field indicates the type of TIM agent. TIMs are used in a variety of settings such as manufacturing facilities, maintenance areas, and storage areas. TIMs are further characterized by using a high, medium, or low hazard index.

Examples of TIMs are ammonia, carbon monoxide, chlorine, hydrogen cyanide, phosgene, and mineral acids (e.g., hydrochloric acid, sulfuric acid, and nitric acid).

3.2.4 Duration of Protection

The Duration of Protection data field indicates the amount of time the equipment provides adequate protection. Since duration varies depending on the concentration of agent, type of agent, and environmental conditions, duration will be given with respect to specific conditions.

3.2.5 Recommended Use(s)

The Recommended Use(s) data field idendifies the areas where the equipment is most likely to be used per vendor or manufacturer recommendation (e.g., tactical operations, and crisis management).

3.3 Physical Parameters Category

The Physical Parameters Category includes the following data fields:

1. Sizes Available.
2. Weight.
3. Package Size and Volume.
4. Power Requirements.
5. Material Type.
6. Construction Type.
7. Color.

Each of these data fields is defined in more detail in the remainder of this section.

3.3.1 Size Available

The Sizes Available data field provides available sizes for an item, to include both male and female when appropriate.

3.3.2 Weight

The Weight data field indicates the total weight of the equipment/system.

3.3.3 Package Size and Volume

The Package Size and Volume data field provides the external dimensions of the system when packaged (for storage and transportability).

3.3.4 Power Requirements

The Power Requirements data field indicates the type of power (ac, dc, etc.) required to operate the equipment. This category applies primarily to respiratory, respiratory support equipment, and heating/cooling systems.

3.3.5 Material Type

The Material Type data field refers to the material content of the respiratory protection apparatus.

3.3.6 Construction Type

The Construction Type data field indicates how the protective apparatus is formed.

3.3.7 Color

The Color data field indicates if equipment has camouflage capability (signature reduction). Color can help identify job type.

3.4 Logistical Parameters Category

The Logistical Parameters Category includes the following data fields:

1. Ease of Use.
2. Consumables.
3. Maintenance Requirements.
4. Shelf Life.
5. Transportability.
6. Operational Limitations.
7. Environmental Conditions.
8. Unit Cost.
9. Maintenance Cost.
10. Warranty.
11. Don/Doff Information.
12. Use/Reuse.
13. Launderability.
14. Accessories.

Each of these data fields is defined in more detail in the remainder of this section.

3.4.1 Ease of Use

Ease of Use is the mobility and flexibility of an individual while wearing the equipment as well as the compatibility of the equipment with other equipment.

3.4.2 Consumables

Consumables are the supplies used during operation and storage. Examples of consumables are batteries, canisters, hoses, etc.

3.4.3 Maintenance Requirements

Maintenance Requirements are the services and parts required to keep the system at its peak operational readiness (e.g., preventative maintenance) and the frequency of required maintenance (e.g., after use, quarterly, and annually).

3.4.4 Shelf Life

Shelf Life is the length of time a piece of equipment can be stored before it needs to be replaced. Shelf life includes the recommended storage procedure and any factors that decrease shelf life (e.g., UV, and critical temperature).

3.4.5 Transportability

Transportability is the ability of the equipment to be transported, including any support equipment (e.g., respiratory equipment and heating/cooling systems).

3.4.6 Operational Limitations

Operational Limitations refer to the length of time responders can safely work at various temperatures (i.e., 50 °F, 70 °F, and 90 °F) and the availability/compatibility of cooling systems to help manage heat stress.

3.4.7 Environmental Conditions

Environmental Conditions indicate whether the equipment is designed for use in all common outdoor weather conditions and climates (e.g., rain, snow, extreme temperatures, and humidity) or only under relatively controlled conditions.

3.4.8 Unit Cost

Unit Cost is the cost of a complete system, including support equipment and operating costs (i.e., consumables).

3.4.9 Maintenance Cost

Maintenance Cost is the cost required to maintain the system at its operational readiness. This cost will be based on equipment usage rates.

3.4.10 Warranty

The Warranty is the length of time a piece of equipment is guaranteed by the manufacturer, including the terms of the warranty (parts and labor).

3.4.11 Don/Doff Information

The Don/Doff Information indicates whether the system requires assistance for donning and/or doffing and the average time for this activity.

3.4.12 Use/Reuse

Use/Reuse indicates the need for any part of the equipment to be discarded after use or its ability to be reused. The data field includes the procedures used to decontaminate and/or dispose of used equipment.

3.4.13 Launderability

Launderability includes the cleaning procedures that are safe for the item, including the number of times the item can be cleaned and remain effective. Also, launderability includes any special procedures needed for specific components.

3.4.14 Accessories

Accessories include those items that are provided with the basic equipment.

3.5 Special Requirements Category

The Special Requirements category includes the following data fields:

1. Training Requirements.
2. Training Available.
3. Manuals Available.
4. Surveillance Testing Requirements.
5. Support Equipment.
6. Testing Information.
7. Applicable Regulations.
8. Health Hazards.
9. Communications Interface Capability.
10. EOD Compatibility.

Each of these data fields is defined in more detail in the remainder of this section.

3.5.1 Training Requirements

The Training Requirements data field refers to the amount of instruction time the operator needs to become proficient in using a piece of equipment.

3.5.2 Training Available

The Training Available data field refers to training available from the manufacturer. This includes any initial training and recertification training that is available.

3.5.3 Manuals Available

The Manuals Available data field indicates the types of manuals available from the manufacturer (e.g., user manuals, and training documentation).

3.5.4 Surveillance Testing Requirements

The Surveillance Testing Requirements data field specifies the testing required to keep a piece of equipment at its operational readiness (e.g., inspecting respiratory masks or suits for holes or tears).

3.5.5 Support Equipment

The Support Equipment data field refers to any additional equipment required to operate the primary unit.

3.5.6 Testing Information

The Testing Information data field includes any test data obtained from the manufacturer and other sources regarding any part of the equipment (e.g., validation testing including materials and ensemble testing such as abrasion, tear, wear, burst, and permeation testing).

3.5.7 Applicable Regulations

The Applicable Regulations data field includes any government and/or safety regulations that may apply to the possession, use, or storage of any part of the system.

3.5.8 Health Hazards

The Health Hazards data field identifies all materials that possess a potential health hazard.

3.5.9 Communications Interface Capability

The Communications Interface Capability data field refers to the ability of the personal protective equipment to interface with a communications system (network capability, hardwire capability, and RF communication).

3.5.10 EOD Compatibility

The EOD Compatibility data field is the ability of the equipment to be used with EOD systems (i.e., suits). For example, a CB protective suit and respirator are required to be worn with an EOD suit in a CB environment.

APPENDIX A—REFERENCES

APPENDIX A—REFERENCES

1. Armando S. Bevelacqua and Richard H. Stilp, *Terrorism Handbook for Operational Responders*, Emergency Film Group, Edgartown, MA, January 1998.

2. Robert E. Hunt, Timothy Hayes, and Warren B. Carroll, *Guidelines for Mass Casualty Decontamination During a Terrorist Chemical Agent Incident*, Battelle, Columbus, OH, September 1999.

3. A.K. Stuempfle, D.J. Howells, S.J. Armour, and C.A. Boulet, *International Task Force 25: Hazard from Industrial Chemicals Final Report*, Edgewood Research Development and Engineering Center, Aberdeen Proving Ground, MD, AD-B236562, ERDEC-SP-061, April 1998.

4. *Responding to a Biological or Chemical Threat: A Practical Guide*, U.S. Department of State, Bureau of Diplomatic Security, Washington, DC, 1996.

5. *2000 Emergency Response Guidebook, A Guidebook for First Responders During the Initial Phase of a Dangerous Goods/Hazardous Materials Incident*, U.S. Department of Transportation, Research and Special Programs Administration, Tempest Publishing, Alexandria, VA, January 2000.

6. *Potential Military Chemical/Biological Agents and Compounds*, FM 3-9, AFR 355-7, NAVFAC P-467, Army Chemical School, Fort McClellan, AL, December 12, 1990.

7. *Journal of the International Society for Respiratory Protection*, Vol. 17, Issue III, Fall 1999.

8 *Guidelines for Incident Commander's Use of Firefighter Protective Ensemble (FFPE) with Self Contained Breathing Apparatus (SCBA) for Rescue Operations During a Terrorist Chemical Agent Incident*, U.S. Army Soldier and Biological Chemical Command (SBCCOM) Domestic Preparedness Chemical Team, Aberdeen Proving Ground, MD, April 30, 1999.

9. Lee E. Campbell, Ray Lins, and Alex G. Pappas, *Domestic Preparedness: Sarin Vapor Challenge and Corn Oil Protection Factor (PF) Testing of 3M BE10 Powered Air Purifying Respirator (PAPR) with AP3 Cartridge*, Soldier and Biological Chemical Command (SBCCOM), AMSSB-REN, Aberdeen Proving Ground, MD, January 2001.

APPENDIX B—INDEX BY RESPIRATORY PROTECTIVE EQUIPMENT IDENTIFICATION NUMBER

Index by Respiratory Protective Equipment Identification Number

ID #	Respiratory PPE Name	Manufacturer	Page E-#
1	Avon CT12 Special Forces Respirator	Avon Technical Products Protection Group	1
2	NBC FM12 Respirator	Avon Technical Products Protection Group	3
3	NBC SF10 Respirator	Avon Technical Products Protection Group	6
4	Avon NBC-SCBA-Option	Avon Technical Products Protection Group	8
5	NBC CoolAir SCBA	Aerospace Design and Development	11
6	SuperCritical Air Mobility Pack (SCAMP®) Self Contained Breathing Apparatus (SCBA)	Aerospace Design and Development	13
7	Biomarine BioPak 60 Rebreather	Biomarine Inc., A Neutronics Company	15
8	Biomarine BioPak 240 Repreather	Biomarine Inc., A Neutronics Company	18
9	Bullard CC20 Series Airline Respirator	Bullard	21
10	Bullard Spectrum-PDE Pressure Demand Respirator with ESCBA	Bullard	24
11	Sabre Tornado® Respiratory System (Airline)	Bullard	26
12	Sabre Tornado® Respiratory System (PAPR)	Bullard	28
13	SR-100, 60 Minute ESCBA	CSE Corporation	30
14	AirBoss PSS100 with Flashing Gauge or with Sentinel	Draeger Safety, Inc.	32
15	AirBoss Evolution with Flashing Gauge or with Sentinal	Draeger Safety, Inc.	35
16	BG-4 w/Mask	Draeger Safety, Inc.	38
17	ProAir Evolution	Draeger Safety, Inc.	40
18	Panorama Nova Full Facepiece	Draeger Safety, Inc.	43
19	Parat NBC Escape Hood	Draeger Safety, Inc.	45
20	Kareta M Mask	Draeger Safety, Inc.	47
21	Duram Emergency Escape Respirator	Duram Rubber Products, Israel	49
22	PP mask with ABP3/US canister	GIAT Industries, France	52
23	PAPR system	GIAT Industries, France	54
24	EVATOX Adult Escape Hood US	GIAT Industries, France	56
25	M40 Series Gas Mask	ILC Dover, Inc.	58

ID #	Respiratory PPE Name	Manufacturer	Page E–#
26	M42 Series Gas Mask	ILC Dover, Inc.	61
27	ARAP/C and ARAP/E Airline Respirators	International Safety Instruments	64
28	Viking Digital SCBA	International Safety Instruments	66
29	Interspiro Spiroscape Escape BA	Interspiro Group	68
30	Interspiro Respirator	Interspiro Group	71
31	C4 Gas Mask	Irvin Aerospace Canada Limited	73
32	Litpac II-Rebreather	Litton Life Support	75
33	Easiflow Plus Full Facemask Respirator and Filters	Martindale Centurion Safety Products Ltd.	79
34	Magnum 4000 P3, with Full Facemask	Martindale Centurion Safety Products Ltd.	81
35	Magnum 4500 P3, with Full Facemask	Martindale Centurion Safety Products Ltd.	83
36	Magnum 8000 P3, with Full Facemask	Martindale Centurion Safety Products Ltd.	85
37	Magnum 8500 P3, with Full Facemask	Martindale Centurion Safety Products Ltd.	87
38	9 mtr Unpowered Fresh-Air Hose System	Martindale Centurion Safety Products Ltd.	89
39	M95 Respirator NBC Protective Respirator	Micronel Safety	91
40	MSA Advantage 1000 CBA/RCA Full-Face Respirator	MSA	94
41	MSA Advantage 1000 with GME-P100 Cartridges	MSA	97
42	MSA Millennium Chemical-Biological Mask	MSA	100
43	MSA OptimAir® MM 2K PAPR	MSA	103
44	MSA OptimAir* 6A PAPR with OptiFilter Cartridges	MSA	106
45	MSA Phalanx CBA/RCA Gas Mask	MSA	109
46	MSA PremAire™ XV Supplied Air Respirator	MSA	112
47	MSA RescueAire™ II Portable Air-Supply System	MSA	114
48	MSA Ultra-Twin® Respirators	MSA	117
49	MSA MCU-2/P and MCU-2A/P Series	MSA	120
50	MSA MMR Xtreme® Air Mask	MSA	123
51	3M™ Breathe Easy™ Powered Air Purifying Respirator System	3M	126

ID #	Respiratory PPE Name	Manufacturer	Page E-#
52	3M™ Breathe Easy™ Powered Air Purifying Respirator System	3M	129
53	3M™ 5000 Series Full Facepiece Respirators	3M	132
54	3M™ 6000 Series Full Facepiece Respirator	3M	134
55	3M™ 7800S-BA Full Facepiece Respirators	3M	136
56	3M™ SCBAG Self-Contained Breathing Apparatus	3M	138
57	3M™ Belt-Mounted PAPR	3M	141
58	3M™ GVP Belt-Mounted Powered Air Purifying Respirator	3M	143
59	3M™ Escort Combination ESCBA/Supplied Air Respirator	3M	145
60	3M™ Full Facepiece FR-M40	3M	147
61	Scott AV 2000 AV-2000® Facepiece	Scott Health and Safety	150
62	Scott C420 Variflo™ PAPR	Scott Health and Safety	152
63	PAN1 Dual Cartridge Full Face Respirator	Shalon Chemical Industries Ltd., Israel	154
64	PAN2 Single Filter Canister	Shalon Chemical Industries Ltd., Israel	157
65	Model 4A1 NBC Respirator	Shalon Chemical Industries Ltd., Israel	160
66	M15-A30 NBC Respirator	Shalon Chemical Industries Ltd., Israel	163
67	SE400 Fan Supplied, Positive Pressure Respirator (FPBR)	SEA	166
68	Survivair™ Cougar SCBA	Survivair	169
69	Survivair™ Belt Mounted PAPR	Survivair	172

APPENDIX C—INDEX BY RESPIRATORY PROTECTIVE EQUIPMENT NAME

Index by Respiratory Protective Equipment Name

Respiratory PPE Name	Manufacturer	ID #	Page E-#
3M™ 5000 Series Full Facepiece Respirators	3M	53	132
3M™ 6000 Series Full Facepiece Respirator	3M	54	134
3M™ 7800S-BA Full Facepiece Respirators	3M	55	136
3M™ Belt-Mounted PAPR	3M	57	141
3M™ Breathe Easy™ Powered Air Purifying Respirator System	3M	51	126
3M™ Breathe Easy™ Powered Air Purifying Respirator System	3M	52	129
3M™ Escort Combination ESCBA/Supplied Air Respirator	3M	59	145
3M™ Full Facepiece FR-M40	3M	60	147
3M™ GVP Belt-Mounted Powered Air Purifying Respirator	3M	58	143
3M™ SCBAG Self-Contained Breathing Apparatus	3M	56	138
9 mtr Unpowered Fresh-Air Hose System	Martindale Centurion Safety Products Ltd.	38	89
AirBoss Evolution with Flashing Gauge or with Sentinal	Draeger Safety, Inc.	15	35
AirBoss PSS100 with Flashing Gauge or with Sentinel	Draeger Safety, Inc.	14	32
ARAP/C and ARAP/E Airline Respirators	International Safety Instruments	27	64
Avon CT12 Special Forces Respirator	Avon Technical Products Protection Group	1	1
Avon NBC-SCBA-Option	Avon Technical Products Protection Group	4	8
BG-4 w/Mask	Draeger Safety, Inc.	16	38
Biomarine BioPak 240 Repreather	Biomarine Inc., A Neutronics Company	8	18
Biomarine BioPak 60 Rebreather	Biomarine Inc., A Neutronics Company	7	15
Bullard CC20 Series Airline Respirator	Bullard	9	21
Bullard Spectrum-PDE Pressure Demand Respirator with ESCBA	Bullard	10	24
C4 Gas Mask	Irvin Aerospace Canada Ltd.	31	73
Duram Emergency Escape Respirator	Duram Rubber Products, Israel	21	49

Respiratory PPE Name	Manufacturer	ID #	Page E-#
Easiflow Plus Full Facemask Respirator and Filters	Martindale Centurion Safety Products Ltd.	33	79
EVATOX Adult Escape Hood US	GIAT Industries, France	24	56
Interspiro Respirator	Interspiro Group	30	71
Interspiro Spiroscape Escape BA	Interspiro Group	29	68
Kareta M Mask	Draeger Safety, Inc.	20	47
Litpac II-Rebreather	Litton Life Support	32	75
M15-A30 NBC Respirator	Shalon Chemical Industries Ltd., Israel	66	163
M40 Series Gas Mask	ILC Dover, Inc.	25	58
M42 Series Gas Mask	ILC Dover, Inc.	26	61
M95 Respirator NBC Protective Respirator	Micronel Safety	39	91
Magnum 4000 P3, with Full Facemask	Martindale Centurion Safety Products Ltd.	34	81
Magnum 4500 P3, with Full Facemask	Martindale Centurion Safety Products Ltd.	35	83
Magnum 8000 P3, with Full Facemask	Martindale Centurion Safety Products Ltd.	36	85
Magnum 8500 P3, with Full Facemask	Martindale Centurion Safety Products Ltd.	37	87
Model 4A1 NBC Respirator (69)	Shalon Chemical Industries Ltd., Israel	65	160
MSA Advantage 1000 CBA/RCA Full-Face Respirator	MSA	40	94
MSA Advantage 1000 with GME-P100 Cartridges	MSA	41	97
MSA MCU-2/P and MCU-2A/P Series	MSA	49	120
MSA Millennium Chemical-Biological Mask	MSA	42	100
MSA MMR Xtreme® Air Mask	MSA	50	123
MSA OptimAir* 6A PAPR with OptiFilter Cartridges	MSA	44	106
MSA OptimAir® MM 2K PAPR	MSA	43	103
MSA Phalanx CBA/RCA Gas Mask	MSA	45	109
MSA PremAire™ XV Supplied Air Respirator	MSA	46	112
MSA RescueAire™ II Portable Air-Supply System	MSA	47	114
MSA Ultra-Twin® Respirators	MSA	48	117

Respiratory PPE Name	Manufacturer	ID #	Page E-#
NBC CoolAir SCBA	Aerospace Design and Development	5	11
NBC FM12 Respirator	Avon Technical Products Protection Group	2	3
NBC SF10 Respirator	Avon Technical Products Protection Group	3	6
PAN1 Dual Cartridge Full Face Respirator	Shalon Chemical Industries Ltd., Israel	63	154
PAN2 Single Filter Canister	Shalon Chemical Industries Ltd., Israel	64	157
Panorama Nova Full Facepiece	Draeger Safety, Inc.	18	43
Parat NBC Escape Hood	Draeger Safety, Inc.	19	45
PAPR System	GIAT Industries, France	23	54
PP mask with ABP3/US canister	GIAT Industries, France	22	52
ProAir Evolution	Draeger Safety, Inc.	17	40
Sabre Tornado® Respiratory System (Airline)	Bullard	11	26
Sabre Tornado® Respiratory System (PAPR)	Bullard	12	28
Scott AV 2000 AV-2000® Facepiece	Scott Health and Safety	61	150
Scott C420 Variflo™ PAPR	Scott Health and Safety	62	152
SE400 Fan Supplied, Positive Pressure Respirator (FPBR)	SEA	67	166
SR-100, 60 Minute ESCBA	CSE Corporation	13	30
SuperCritical Air Mobility Pack (SCAMP®) Self Contained Breathing Apparatus (SCBA)	Aerospace Design and Development	6	13
Survivair™ Belt Mounted PAPR	Survivair	69	172
Survivair™ Cougar SCBA	Survivair	68	169
Viking Digital SCBA	International Safety Instruments	28	66

APPENDIX D—INDEX BY RESPIRATORY PROTECTIVE EQUIPMENT MANUFACTURER

Index by Respiratory Protective Equipment Manufacturer

Manufacturer	Respiratory PPE Name	ID #	Page E-#
3M	3M™ Full Facepiece FR-M40	60	147
3M	3M™ Breathe Easy™ Powered Air Purifying Respirator System	51	126
3M	3M™ Breathe Easy™ Powered Air Purifying Respirator System	52	129
3M	3M™ 5000 Series Full Facepiece Respirators	53	132
3M	3M™ 6000 Series Full Facepiece Respirator	54	134
3M	3M™ 7800S-BA Full Facepiece Respirators	55	136
3M	3M™ SCBAG Self-Contained Breathing Apparatus	56	138
3M	3M™ Belt-Mounted PAPR	57	141
3M	3M™ GVP Belt-Mounted Powered Air Purifying Respirator	58	143
3M	3M™ Escort Combination ESCBA/Supplied Air Respirator	59	145
Aerospace Design and Development	NBC CoolAir SCBA	5	11
Aerospace Design and Development	SuperCritical Air Mobility Pack (SCAMP®) Self Contained Breathing Apparatus	6	13
Avon Technical Products Protection Group	Avon CT12 Special Forces Respirator	1	1
Avon Technical Products Protection Group	NBC FM12 Respirator	2	3
Avon Technical Products Protection Group	NBC SF10 Respirator	3	6
Avon Technical Products Protection Group	Avon NBC-SCBA-Option	4	8
Biomarine Inc., A Neutronics Company	Biomarine BioPak 60 Rebreather	7	15
Biomarine Inc., A Neutronics Company	Biomarine BioPak 240 Repreather	8	18
Bullard	Bullard CC20 Series Airline Respirator	9	21
Bullard	Bullard Spectrum-PDE Pressure Demand Respirator with ESCBA	10	24
Bullard	Sabre Tornado® Respiratory System (Airline)	11	26
Bullard	Sabre Tornado® Respiratory System	12	28

Manufacturer	Respiratory PPE Name	ID #	Page E–#
	(PAPR)		
CSE Corporation	SR-100, 60 Minute ESCBA	13	30
Draeger Safety, Inc.	AirBoss PSS100 with Flashing Gauge or with Sentinel	14	32
Draeger Safety, Inc.	AirBoss Evolution with Flashing Gauge or with Sentinal	15	35
Draeger Safety, Inc.	BG-4 w/Mask	16	38
Draeger Safety, Inc.	ProAir Evolution	17	40
Draeger Safety, Inc.	Panorama Nova Full Facepiece	18	43
Draeger Safety, Inc.	Parat NBC Escape Hood	19	45
Draeger Safety, Inc.	Kareta M Mask	20	47
Duram Rubber Products, Israel	Duram Emergency Escape Respirator	21	49
GIAT Industries, France	EVATOX Adult Escape Hood US	24	56
GIAT Industries, France	PAPR System	23	54
GIAT Industries, France	PP Mask with ABP3/US Canister	22	52
ILC Dover, Inc.	M40 Series Gas Mask	25	58
ILC Dover, Inc.	M42 Series Gas Mask	26	61
International Safety Instruments	ARAP/C and ARAP/E Airline Respirators	27	64
International Safety Instruments	Viking Digital SCBA	28	66
Interspiro Group	Interspiro Spiroscape Escape BA	29	68
Interspiro Group	Interspiro Respirator	30	71
Irvin Aerospace Canada Ltd.	C4 Gas Mask	31	73
Litton Life Support	Litpac II-Rebreather	32	75
Martindale Centurion Safety Products Ltd.	Easiflow Plus Full Facemask Respirator and Filters	33	79
Martindale Centurion Safety Products Ltd.	Magnum 4000 P3, with Full Facemask	34	81
Martindale Centurion Safety Products Ltd.	Magnum 4500 P3, with Full Facemask	35	83
Martindale Centurion Safety Products Ltd.	Magnum 8000 P3, with Full Facemask	36	85
Martindale Centurion Safety Products Ltd.	9 mtr Unpowered Fresh-Air Hose System	38	89
Martindale Centurion Safety Products Ltd.	Magnum 8500 P3, with Full Facemask	37	87
Micronel Safety	M95 Respirator NBC Protective Respirator	39	91
MSA	MSA Advantage 1000 CBA/RCA Full-Face Respirator	40	94
MSA	MSA Advantage 1000 with GME-P100 Cartridges	41	97
MSA	MSA Millennium Chemical-Biological	42	100

Manufacturer	Respiratory PPE Name	ID #	Page E-#
	Mask		
MSA	MSA OptimAir® MM 2K PAPR	43	103
MSA	MSA OptimAir* 6A PAPR with OptiFilter Cartridges	44	106
MSA	MSA Phalanx CBA/RCA Gas Mask	45	109
MSA	MSA PremAire™ XV Supplied Air Respirator	46	112
MSA	MSA RescueAire™ II Portable Air-Supply System	47	114
MSA	MSA Ultra-Twin® Respirators	48	117
MSA	MSA MCU-2/P and MCU-2A/P Series	49	120
MSA	MSA MMR Xtreme® Air Mask	50	123
Scott Health & Safety	Scott AV 2000 AV-2000® Facepiece	61	150
Scott Health & Safety	Scott C420 Variflo™ PAPR	62	152
SEA	SE400 Fan Supplied, Positive Pressure Respirator (FPBR)	67	166
Shalon Chemical Industries Ltd., Israel	PAN1 Dual Cartridge Full Face Respirator	63	154
Shalon Chemical Industries Ltd., Israel	PAN2 Single Filter Canister	64	157
Shalon Chemical Industries Ltd., Israel	Model 4A1 NBC Respirator (69)	65	160
Shalon Chemical Industries Ltd., Israel	M15-A30 NBC Respirator	66	163

APPENDIX E—RESPIRATORY PROTECTIVE EQUIPMENT DATA SHEETS

Personal Protective Equipment (Respiratory)

General

Name
ID# 1

Avon CT12 Special Forces Respirator

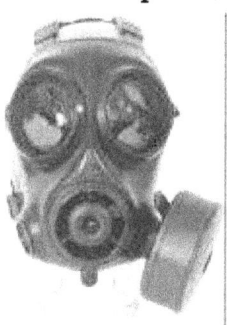

Technology Respirator; designed to provide respiratory, eye, and face protection

Stock Number
Size 1: 70046/18/1
Size 2: 70046/18/2
Size 3: 70046/18/3

Protection Type Respiratory and percutaneous (CT12)

Equipment Category Respirator, canister

Availability In production since 1995

Current User(s) Various police forces and security services in USA and worldwide

Manufacturer
Avon Technical Products Protection Group
Bathroad, Melksham, Wiltshire SN12 8AA
Contact: Mr. M. Hoban
+44 (0) 1225 896375 (Tel)

Manufacturer Type Foreign

Developer Avon Technical Products Protection Group

Source
The JGW Group
10640 Main Street
Suite 200
Fairfax, VA 22030
703-352-3400 (Tel)
POC: Jack O'Neil
e-mail: joneil@jgwgroup.com
website: www.jgwgroup.com
Safety Systems Inc.
630-653-1103 (Tel)
POC: Charlie Bicek

Certification CT12/CTF12: NIOSH approval number TC-14G-0255 (August 9, 1999)
CT12/DPF12: NIOSH approval in process for CW/BW/TIMs protection

Operational Parameters

Chemical Warfare (CW) Agents Protected Against
Not CW agents (unless fitted with full NBC filter)
NIOSH approval in process for CT12 with DPF12 filter

Biological Warfare (BW) Agents Protected Against
Not suitable (unless fitted with full NBC filter)
NIOSH approval in process for CT12 with DPF12 filter

Toxic Industrial Materials (TIMs) Protected Against
Riot control agents, CS, CN, OC (when fitted with CTF12 filter)
NIOSH approval in process for CT12 with DPF12 filter

Duration of Protection	Depends on exposure time and challenge concentration
Recommended Use(s)	Riot control

Physical Parameters

Sizes Available	Small, medium, and large
Weight	1 lb without filter and 1.4 lb with filter
Package Size and Volume	370 cu in per unit (packed singly)
Power Requirements	None
Material Type	Impermeable butyl rubber facepiece, polycarbonate eyepiece, and fabric head harness
Construction Type	Molded rubber facepiece and polycarbonate eyepiece
Color	Black

Logistical Parameters

Ease of Use	Easy to put on and remove mask; easy to clean; compatible with other equipment. Sight correction available for standard mask. Very low breathing resistance.
Consumables	CTF12 filter (future: DPF12 filter)
Maintenance Requirements	Cleaning and disinfection
Shelf Life	7 yr to 10 yr
Transportability	No special requirements. Easily transported.
Operational Limitations	Not specified
Environmental Conditions	Designed to operate under all environmental conditions: artic to tropic and/or jungle. Not for underwater use.
Unit Cost	Not specified
Maintenance Cost	Maintenance and repair at unit level. Spares and toolkit are available.
Warranty	1 yr
Don/Doff Information	None required
Use/Reuse	Mask: clean and reuse. Filter: dispose (consumable).
Launderability	Clean in mild disinfectant and hot soapy water
Accessories	Filter and carrier

Special Requirements

Training Requirements	1/2 h of training is required
Training Available	Maintenance training is available
Manuals Available	User manual
Surveillance Testing Requirements	Inspection after cleaning. Approval inspection of valves.
Support Equipment	CTF12 filter
Testing Information	Available from Avon upon request
Applicable Regulations	NIOSH and OSHA
Health Hazards	None
Communications Interface Capability	Not specified
EOD Compatibility	Not specified

General

Name
ID# 2

NBC FM12 Respirator

Technology   Respirator; canister (left and right handed canister mountings)

Stock Number   AMF12 (canister) 4240–21–912–5397
Dutch:
Size 1: 4240–99–882–1553
Size 2: 4240–99–062–2181
Size 3: 4240–99–501–1596
Denmark:
Size 1: 4240–99–888–3404
Size 2: 4240–99–330–1579
Size 3: 4240–99–219–2665
Norway:
Size 1: 4240–99–215–9778
Size 2: 4240–99–547–8423
Size 3: 4240–99–662–8071

Protection Type   Respiratory (FM12)

Equipment Category Respirator and canister

Availability   In production since 1992

Current User(s)   Norwegian, Danish, Dutch, Portugal, and Singapore Defense Forces

Manufacturer   Avon Technical Products Protection Group
Bathroad, Melksham, Wiltshire SN12 8AA
POC: Mr. M. Hoban
+44 (0) 1225 896375 (Tel)

Manufacturer Type   Foreign

Developer   Avon Technical Products Protection Group

Source   The JGW Group
10640 Main Street
Suite 200
Fairfax, VA 22030
703–352–3400 (Tel)
POC: Jack O'Neil
e-mail: joneil@jgwgroup.com
website: www.jgwgroup.com
Safety Systems Inc.
630–653–1103 (Tel)
POC: Charlie Bicek

Certification   FM12/AMF12: Approved by Defense Departments of National Customers
by NATO Triptych
FM12/CT12: NIOSH approval number TC–14G–0255 (November 15, 2000)

FM12/DP12: NIOSH approval in process for CW/BW/TIMs protection

Operational Parameters

Chemical Warfare (CW) Agents Protected Against
All classical CW agents (when fitted with AMF12 or C2A1 NBC filter; or DPF12 filter in future)

Biological Warfare (BW) Agents Protected Against
All classical BW agents (when fitted with AMF12 or C2A1 NBC filter, or DPF12 filter in future)

Toxic Industrial Materials (TIMs) Protected Against
Protection against riot control agents, organic vapors and acid gases (when fitted with CTF12 filter or future DPF12 filter)

Duration of Protection
Depends on exposure time and challenge concentration

Recommended Use(s)
Riot control

Physical Parameters

Sizes Available
Small, medium, and large

Weight
1 lb without filter and 1.6 lb with filter

Package Size and Volume
370 cu in per unit (packed singly)

Power Requirements
None

Material Type
Impermeable butyl rubber facepiece, polycarbonate eyepiece, and fabric head harness

Construction Type
Molded rubber facepiece and polycarbonate eyepiece

Color
Black

Logistical Parameters

Ease of Use
Easy to put on and remove mask; easy to clean; compatible with other equipment. Sight correction available for standard mask. Very low breathing resistance.

Consumables
CTF12, AMF12, or C2A1 NBC Filters (MSA and Racal) or DPF12 (future)

Maintenance Requirements
Cleaning and disinfection

Shelf Life
7 yr to 10 yr

Transportability
No special requirements. Easily transported.

Operational Limitations
Not specified

Environmental Conditions
Designed to operate under all environmental conditions: artic to tropic/jungle. Not for underwater use.

Unit Cost
Not specified

Maintenance Cost
Not specified

Warranty
1 yr

Don/Doff Information
None required

Use/Reuse
Mask: clean and reuse. Filter: dispose (consumable).

Launderability
Clean in mild disinfectant and hot soapy water

Accessories
Filter and carrier; high flow fail-safe drinking system

Special Requirements

Training Requirements
1/2 h of training is required

Training Available
Maintenance training is available

Manuals Available
User manual

Surveillance Testing Requirements
Inspection after cleaning. Approval inspection of valves.

Support Equipment
CTF12, AMF12, or C2A1 filters (future DPF12 filter)

Testing Information	Available from Avon upon request
Applicable Regulations	NIOSH and OSHA
Health Hazards	Environmental considerations: Filter contains metals (copper/2inl). Dispose in accordance with local regulations.
Communications Interface Capability	Optional secondary speech transmitter to allow use of communications equipment
EOD Compatibility	Not specified

General
Name
ID# 3

NBC SF10 Respirator

Technology   Respirator; a cheek mounted screw-in plug gives access to a second canister mount allowing the use of an air-escape bottle for conditions of oxygen depletion. Low profile coated polycarbonate eyepieces with enhanced impact resistance.

Stock Number   Size 1: 4240-99-146-7929
                        Size 2: 4240-99-774-1621
                        Size 3: 4240-99-083-1292
                        Size 4: 4240-99-785-7309

Protection Type   Respiratory (SF10)
Equipment Category   Respirator and canister
Availability   Commercially available
Current User(s)   British Armed Forces. Special Forces in UK and USA.
Manufacturer   Avon Technical Products
                        Protection Group
                        Bathroad, Melksham, Wiltshire SN12 8AA
                        POC: Mr. M. Hoban
                        +44 (0) 1225 896375 (Tel)
Manufacturer Type   Foreign

Developer   Avon Technical Products Protection Group

Source   The JGW Group
                        10640 Main Street
                        Suite 200
                        Fairfax, VA 22030
                        703-352-3400 (Tel)
                        POC: Jack O'Neil
                        e-mail: joneil@jgwgroup.com
                        website: www.jgwgroup.com
                        Safety Systems Inc.
                        630-653-1103 (Tel)
                        POC: Charlie Bicek
Certification   SF10/RC670: NIOSH number TC-14G-177 (November 12, 1993)

Operational Parameters
  Chemical Warfare (CW)   Not CW agents (unless fitted with NBC filter)
  Agents Protected Against
  Biological Warfare (BW)   Not suitable (unless fitted with full NBC filter)
  Agents Protected Against
  Toxic Industrial Materials Riot control agents, CS, and CN (when fitted with RC670 filter)
  (TIMs) Protected Against

Duration of Protection	Depends on exposure time and challenge concentration
Recommended Use(s)	Riot control

Physical Parameters

Sizes Available	XS through L
Weight	1.1 lb without filter and 1.5 lb without filter
Package Size and Volume	370 cu in per unit (packed singly)
Power Requirements	None
Material Type	Impermeable butyl rubber facepiece, and fabric head harness. Eyepieces: Low profile coated polycarbonate eyepieces with enhanced impact resistance.
Construction Type	Molded rubber facepiece. Secondary tinted lenses that fit to the outside of the respirator providing additional protection against flash and fragments.
Color	Black

Logistical Parameters

Ease of Use	Easy to put on and remove mask; easy to clean; compatible with other equipment. Sight correction available for standard mask. Very low breathing resistance.
Consumables	Filters
Maintenance Requirements	Cleaning and disinfection
Shelf Life	7 yr to 10 yr
Transportability	No special requirements. Easily transported.
Operational Limitations	Not specified
Environmental Conditions	Designed to operate under all environmental conditions: artic to tropic/jungle. Not for underwater use.
Unit Cost	Not specified
Maintenance Cost	Maintenance and repair at unit level. Spares and toolkit are available.
Warranty	1 yr
Don/Doff Information	None required
Use/Reuse	Mask: clean and reuse. Filter: dispose (consumable).
Launderability	Clean in mild disinfectant and hot soapy water
Accessories	Filter and carrier

Special Requirements

Training Requirements	1/2 h of training is required
Training Available	Maintenance training is available
Manuals Available	User manual
Surveillance Testing Requirements	Inspection after cleaning. Approval inspection of valves.
Support Equipment	RC 670 CS filter canister. Canister thread: NATO standard (STANAG 4155)
Testing Information	Available from Avon upon request
Applicable Regulations	NIOSH and OSHA
Health Hazards	None
Communications Interface Capability	Not specified
EOD Compatibility	Not specified

General

Name

ID# 4

Avon NBC-SCBA-Option

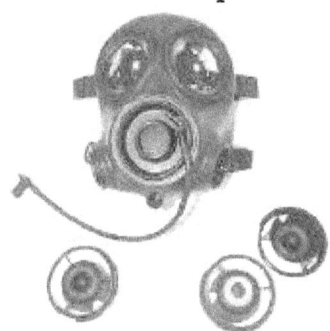

Technology

The S10, SF10, CT12, or FM12 mask may be changed from negative to positive pressure simply by exchanging the standard front cover for one containing the biased exhale valve option. In the Avon respirators, the unique folded acoustic horn-shaped primary speech module (PSM) houses the normal exhalation valve within a cone. The outer edge of the cone forms a seat for a second spring-loaded exhalation valve, giving a positively biased exhalation pressure. The front cover of the PSM, suitably modified, provides a simple means of holding the positive pressure exhalation valve in place.

Stock Number

Not specified

Protection Type

Respiratory

Equipment Category

SCBA—a simple modification for the S10 and FM12 families of military respirator that enables the masks to be used with either a conventional filter or a positive pressure demand valve, instantly switching from one to the other.

Availability

In production

Current User(s)

Various police forces and security services in the USA.
Australian Special Forces.

Manufacturer

Avon Technical Products Protection Group
Bathroad, Melksham, Wiltshire SN12 8AA
POC: Mr. M. Hoban
+44-0-1225-896375 (Tel)

Manufacturer Type

Foreign

Developer

Avon Technical Products Protection Group

Source

The JGW Group
10540 Main Street
Suite 200
Fairfax, VA 22030
703-352-3400 (Tel)
POC: Jack O'Neil
Safety Systems Inc.
630-653-1103 (Tel)
POC: Charlie Bicek

Certification

Not specified

Operational Parameters

Chemical Warfare (CW) Agents Protected Against

Not CW agents (unless fitted with full NBC filter, or DPF12 filter in future)

Biological Warfare (BW) Agents Protected Against	Not suitable (unless fitted with full NBC filter, or DPF12 filter in future)
Toxic Industrial Materials (TIMs) Protected Against	Riot control agents, CS, CN, and OC (when fitted with CTF12 filter, or DPF12 filter in future)
Duration of Protection	Depends on exposure time and challenge concentration
Recommended Use(s)	Anti-terrorist operation, hostage retrieval, and in confined space

Physical Parameters

Sizes Available	Not applicable
Weight	Not specified
Package Size and Volume	Not specified
Power Requirements	None
Material Type	Not specified
Construction Type	Not specified
Color	Black

Logistical Parameters

Ease of Use	The positive pressure demand valve has a unique twist and lock connector, whereas the military masks have the standard NATO screw thread. An off-the-shelf adapter enables the demand valve to screw into the standard filter canister thread.
Consumables	Filters
Maintenance Requirements	Cleaning and disinfection
Shelf Life	Not specified
Transportability	No special requirements. Easily transported.
Operational Limitations	Not specified
Environmental Conditions	Designed to operate under all environmental conditions: Artic to tropic and/or jungle. Not for underwater use.
Unit Cost	Not specified
Maintenance Cost	Maintenance and repair at unit level. Spares and toolkit are available.
Warranty	1 yr
Don/Doff Information	None required
Use/Reuse	Mask: clean and reuse. Filter: dispose (consumable).
Launderability	Clean in mild disinfectant and hot soapy water
Accessories	Filter and carrier, secondary speech transmitter (SST); special tool kit required to convert NBC SF10 Respirator

Special Requirements

Training Requirements	1/2 h of training is required
Training Available	Maintenance training is available
Manuals Available	User manual
Surveillance Testing Requirements	Inspection after cleaning. Approval inspection of valves.
Support Equipment	None
Testing Information	Available from Avon upon request
Applicable Regulations	NIOSH and OSHA
Health Hazards	None

Communications Interface Capability	A secondary speech transmitter (SST) is screwed into one port and the filter canister into the other
EOD Compatibility	Not specified

General

Name	*NBC CoolAir SCBA*
ID# 5	
	Picture Not Available
Technology	SCBA feeds at full flow 100 ml at any altitude. Developed to counter the heat stress of operations in a PPE suit.
Stock Number	Not specified
Protection Type	Respiratory
Equipment Category	SCBA with integral cooling suit
Availability	Commercially available
	1 h and 2 h systems available
Current User(s)	NASA and U.S. Navy
Manufacturer	Aerospace Design and Development
	POC: Kristina Gier
	970–535–0385 (Tel)
Manufacturer Type	Domestic
Developer	Aerospace Design and Development
Source	Life Safety Systems
	343 Soquel Ave
	Suite 317
	Santa Cruz, CA 95062
	POC: Bill Conklin
	831–728–9090 (Tel)
	b@lifesafetysys.com
Certification	Not specified

Operational Parameters

Chemical Warfare (CW) Agents Protected Against	Yes (agents not specified)
Biological Warfare (BW) Agents Protected Against	Yes (agents not specified)
Toxic Industrial Materials (TIMs) Protected Against	Not specified
Duration of Protection	1 h and 2 h systems available
Recommended Use(s)	HAZMAT; any decontamination situation.

Physical Parameters

Sizes Available	One size
Weight	28 lb loaded with 1 h air and cooling supply.
Package Size and Volume	23.5 in x 13 in x 5.5 in
Power Requirements	None
Material Type	Not specified
Construction Type	Not specified
Color	Not specified

Logistical Parameters

Ease of Use	No operator controls
Consumables	Oxygen replenishment
Maintenance Requirements	Monthly testing

Shelf Life	5 yr with annual tank test
Transportability	Requires a support vehicle with recharge capability at scene for extended use
Operational Limitations	Not specified
Environmental Conditions	Operates in all environments
Unit Cost	Approximately $55K
Maintenance Cost	Not specified
Warranty	1 yr full warranty and 5 yr labor
Don/Doff Information	Not specified
Use/Reuse	Not specified
Launderability	Not specified
Accessories	Not specified

Special Requirements

Training Requirements	1 h of training is required
Training Available	Yes. At Aerospace, no charge; at user location, $1200 per day per man plus expenses.
Manuals Available	User manual
Surveillance Testing Requirements	Monthly testing
Support Equipment	None
Testing Information	Available from Aerospace Design and Development
Applicable Regulations	Not specified
Health Hazards	Not specified
Communications Interface Capability	Not specified
EOD Compatibility	Not specified

General

Name

SuperCritical Air Mobility Pack (SCAMP*) Self Contained Breathing Apparatus (SCBA)

ID# 6

Picture Not Available

Technology

SCBA feeds at full flow 100 ml at any altitude. Developed to counter the heat stress of operations in a PPE suit.

Stock Number

Not specified

Protection Type

Respiratory

Equipment Category

SCBA and body cooling suit

Availability

Military and commercial

Current User(s)

NASA and U.S. NAVY

Manufacturer

Aerospace Design and Development
POC: Kristina Gier
970–535–0385 (Tel)

Manufacturer Type

Domestic

Developer

Aerospace Design and Development

Source

Life Safety Systems
343 Soquel Ave
Suite 317
Santa Cruz, CA 95062
POC: Bill Conklin
831–728–9090 (Tel)
b@lifesafetysys.com

Certification

Not specified

Operational Parameters

Chemical Warfare (CW) Agents Protected Against

Not specified

Biological Warfare (BW) Agents Protected Against

Any decontamination situation chemical, biological, nuclear, and HAZMAT

Toxic Industrial Materials (TIMs) Protected Against

Any decontamination situation chemical, biological, nuclear, and HAZMAT

Duration of Protection

1 h systems available now. 2 h systems available in six months.

Recommended Use(s)

This product is ideal for use in any contaminated environment for chemical, biological, nuclear, HAZMAT rescues. Lightweight, small profile tank allows rapid access to and egress from confined spaces.

Physical Parameters

Sizes Available

Not specified

Weight

28 lb loaded with 1 h air and cooling supply

Package Size and Volume

23.5 in x 13 in x 5.5 in

Power Requirements

None

Material Type

Not specified

Construction Type

Not specified

Color

Not specified

Logistical Parameters

Ease of Use

No operator controls

Consumables

O2 replenishment

Maintenance Requirements	Monthly testing
Shelf Life	5 yr with annual tank test
Transportability	Recommend 6 unit system with O2 loading system. Requires a support vehicle with recharge capability at scene for extended use.
Operational Limitations	Any decontamination situation chemical, biological, nuclear, and HAZMAT. Rugged heavy duty components.
Environmental Conditions	Not specified
Unit Cost	Approximately $55K dependent on accessories ordered
Maintenance Cost	Quarterly test
Warranty	1 yr full warranty and 5 yr labor
Don/Doff Information	Not specified
Use/Reuse	Not specified
Launderability	Not specified
Accessories	Not specified

Special Requirements

Training Requirements	1 h; SCBA and mask operational knowledge
Training Available	At our location no charge. At your location $1.2K /d per man plus expenses.
Manuals Available	Standard manuals
Surveillance Testing Requirements	Standardized quarterly test
Support Equipment	Not specified
Testing Information	Aerospace Design and Development
Applicable Regulations	None
Health Hazards	Not specified
Communications Interface Capability	Not specified
EOD Compatibility	Not specified

General

Name
ID# 7

Biomarine BioPak 60 Rebreather

Technology

SCBA; closed circuit self-contained breathing apparatus that maintains positive pressure in the mask. It recirculates the major portion of the user's exhaled gas. A small oxygen cylinder provides make-up gas to a breathing chamber. The user inhales the gas into a silicone facepiece. The user's exhaled breath passes through a carbon dioxide absorbent and back into the breathing chamber, where fresh oxygen is added. The replenished gas is now available for the next inhalation.

Stock Number
Not specified

Protection Type
Respiratory

Equipment Category
SCBA, rebreather

Availability
Commercial

Current User(s)
HAZMAT, police and fire, tunneling and mining rescue, Japanese National Police, industrial users to include waste treatment plants, and chemical plants

Manufacturer
Biomarine Inc.
A Neutronics Company
456 Creamery Way
Exton, PA 19341-2532

Manufacturer Type
Domestic

Developer
Biomarine Inc.

Source
www.neutronicsinc.com
POC: Ted Beck
610-524-8800 (Tel)
610-524-8807 (Fax)
e-mail: ted.beck@neutronicsinc.com

Certification
NIOSH/MSHA Certification TC-13F-371 and TC-13F-372 for use in temperatures as low as +15 °F

Operational Parameters

Chemical Warfare (CW) Agents Protected Against
Not specified

Biological Warfare (BW) Agents Protected Against
Not specified

Toxic Industrial Materials (TIMs) Protected Against
System will protect against most TIMs

Duration of Protection
1 h (60 min)

Recommended Use(s)
Hazardous waste remediation, specialty fire fighting applications, mine rescue, and tunnel rescue

Physical Parameters

Sizes Available
One size

Weight
25 lb (11.25 kg)

Package Size and Volume
13.8 in L x 18.5 in H x 6.6 in W

Power Requirements
Not specified

Material Type
High-impact fire-retarding Macralon shell; neoprene hoses; anti-oxidant silicone rubber facepiece; optional fire-resistant aramid harness and straps, and soft pack case

Construction Type
Not applicable

Color
Orange

Logistical Parameters

Ease of Use
Simple to use. All controls and displays are easily accessible. Extremely comfortable, lightweight, long duration, and durable.

Consumables
Sodasorb CO_2 scrubber and oxygen to recharge the cylinders

Maintenance Requirements
Most repairs and testing can be done in the field. User maintenance requirements are minimized.

Shelf Life
20 yr to 25 yr with proper care and maintenance

Transportability
Easily transported

Operational Limitations
1 h

Environmental Conditions
Can be used in all environmental conditions inside a Level A suit. Can be used in most all environmental conditions outside a Level B suit.

Unit Cost
$3.0K, includes mask and case

Maintenance Cost
Maintenance and spare parts are minimal cost

Warranty
3 yr on unit. 1 yr on all rubber parts.

Don/Doff Information
Buddy system recommended. Donning/doffing time approximately 1 min to 3 min (not including Level A suit).

Use/Reuse
CO_2 scrubbing material. (SodaSorb Lime must be discarded after each use. Scrubber assembly is refilled with fresh SodaSorb material after each use). Oxygen cylinder is recharged after each use.

Launderability
Not applicable

Accessories
Not specified

Special Requirements

Training Requirements
User training required (approximately 2 h to 4 h depending on class size). Benchman training required (approximately 4 h) for maintenance personnel only. User recertification/refresher recommended annually. Benchman recertification recommended every 3 yr.

Training Available
Factory authorized training with each purchase. Refresher training by authorized trainers only.

Manuals Available
Yes, for both user and benchman

Surveillance Testing Requirements
Normal turn-around maintenance and visual inspection

Support Equipment
Not specified

Testing Information
Not specified

Applicable Regulations
Not specified

Health Hazards
Not specified

Communications Interface Capability   Not specified

EOD Compatibility   The U.S. Army EOD uses the BioPak 240 under the STEPO Program. The BioPak 240 is used by several bomb squads as well as Tech Escort, OSIA, DC Capitol Police, and others (see current users).

General

Name
ID# 8

Biomarine BioPak 240 Rebreather

Technology

SCBA; closed circuit self-contained breathing apparatus that maintains positive pressure in the mask. It recirculates the major portion of the user's exhaled gas. A small oxygen cylinder provides make-up gas to a breathing chamber. The user inhales the gas into a silicone facepiece. The user's exhaled breath passes through a carbon dioxide absorbent and back into the breathing chamber, where fresh oxygen is added. The replenished gas is now available for the next inhalation.

Stock Number

Not specified

Protection Type

Respiratory

Equipment Category

SCBA/rebreather. The BioPak 240 includes a case, mask, and manual, but the mask must be ordered as a separate line item.

Availability

Commercial

Current User(s)

The BioPak 240 is widely used by the U. S. Government and Military. The BioPak was designed for mine rescue applications in the late 1980s. From its introduction, it has been tested and used in many military and government applications. The following is a partial list of users and applications of the BioPak:

1) Self-Contained Toxic Protection Outfit (STEPO) The BioPak was tested for this program in 1988. The total number of systems to be produced for the STEPO program is 1,350. Their primary user is Army EOD for disposal of Toxic Agents in fifty-three sites throughout the United States and Europe.

2) The On Site Inspection Agency (OSIA) uses systems for inspection during verification of missile treaties in the former Soviet Union.

3) Washington, DC Capitol Police Bomb Squad. Their systems are for protection of the Capitol and associated facilities.

4) Philadelphia City Bomb Squad. Their systems are used in conjunction with the operation of the city's Bomb Squad.

5) Domestic Preparedness/Weapons of Mass Destruction Program: Atlanta, GA; Arlington, VA; San Antonio, TX; Dallas and Ft. Worth, TX; and Jersey City, NJ has purchased and been trained on the BioPak.

6) Duquesne Light Nuclear Power Plant has over 100 systems used in their facility. Their containment building is sub-atmospheric emergency fire fighting, and requires SCBA. The BioPak 240 gives them the long duration required to perform maintenance work. They are approved to use their units for emergency firefighting.

7) Japanese National Police Authority. We modified our standard BioPak 60 to meet their needs in responding to chemical agent events, such as Sarin Gas attacks in subways. After gaining acceptance of our changes to the BioPak 60, we made it our standard unit. The

changes were also adopted by some city fire departments such as Nagoya.

8) The BioPak 240 and 60 are widely used in mining and tunneling.
9) The Boston Fire Department has over 50 BioPak 240 units for tunneling. The Massachusetts State Police has over 80 BioPak 60 units for use in the new Ted Williams tunnel.
10) Government/Military Classified Applications Information on these items are on a need to know basis.
11) Tech Escort. The U.S. Army uses the BioPak 240 for escorting munitions when a long-term breathing apparatus is required.

Manufacturer	Biomarine Inc. A Neutronics Company 456 Creamery Way Exton, PA 19341–2532
Manufacturer Type	Domestic
Developer	Biomarine Inc.
Source	www.neutronicsinc.com POC: Ted Beck 610–524–8800 (Tel) 610–524–8807 (Fax) e-mail: ted.beck@neutronicsinc.com
Certification	NIOSH/MSHA Certification TC–13F–185 and TC–13F–206 for use in temperatures as low as +15 °F

Operational Parameters

Chemical Warfare (CW) Agents Protected Against	The Army version of the BioPak 240 was tested with live agent, Sarin/Mustard liquid and vapor. The entire operational system was subject to 24 h testing with live agent and passed all Army requirements.
Biological Warfare (BW) Agents Protected Against	Not specified
Toxic Industrial Materials (TIMs) Protected Against	Will protect against most TIMS
Duration of Protection	4 h (240 min). It is suggested that each BioPak 240 have a spare oxygen cylinder and coolant canister. This allows the BioPak 240 to be immediately "turned around" after use for an additional 4 h of use.
Recommended Use(s)	Hazardous waste remediation, specialty fire fighting applications, mine rescue, and tunnel rescue.

Physical Parameters

Sizes Available	One size
Weight	35 lb (15.75 kg)
Package Size and Volume	15.8 in L x 24.8 in H x 7.8 in W
Power Requirements	Not specified
Material Type	High-impact fire-retarding NORYL shell; neoprene hoses; anti-oxidant silicone rubber facepiece; optional fire-resistant Kevlar harness and straps, and molded carrying case
Construction Type	Not applicable
Color	Grey

Logistical Parameters

Ease of Use
Simple to use. All controls and displays are easily accessible. Extremely comfortable due to fully padded harness with multiple adjustments, lightweight, long duration, and durable.

Consumables
LimePak CO_2 Scrubber and oxygen to recharge the cylinders. Disinfectant cleaner.

Maintenance Requirements
Requires minimum preparation and set-up time. All testing can be done in the field with a minimum of training.

Shelf Life
20 yr to 25 yr with proper care and maintenance

Transportability
Easily transported

Operational Limitations
It is suggested that each BioPak 240 have a spare oxygen cylinder and coolant canister. This allows the BioPak 240 to be immediately "turned around" after use for an additional 4 h of use.

Environmental Conditions
Can be used in all environmental conditions inside a Level A suit. Can be used in most all environmental conditions outside a Level B suit.

Unit Cost
$5.27K, includes mask and case

Maintenance Cost
Maintenance and spare parts are minimal cost

Warranty
3 yr on unit. 1 yr on all rubber parts.

Don/Doff Information
Buddy system recommended. Donning/doffing time approximately 1 min to 3 min (not including Level A suit).

Use/Reuse
CO_2 scrubbing material. (LimePak must be discarded after each use. Scrubber assembly is refilled with fresh LimePak material after each use). O_2 cylinder is recharged after each use.

Launderability
Not applicable

Accessories
Spare O_2 cylinder and coolant canister, lens insert for clear, fog-free vision for 4 h, and wiper option available.

Special Requirements

Training Requirements
Approximately 2 h to 4 h (depending on class size) of user training required. Benchman training approximately 4 h required for maintenance personnel only. User recertification/refresher recommended annually. Benchman recertification recommended every 3 yr.

Training Available
Factory authorized training with each purchase. Refresher training by authorized trainers only (users can be certified).

Manuals Available
Yes, for both user and benchman

Surveillance Testing Requirements
Normal turn-around maintenance and visual inspection

Support Equipment
"Blue-ice" insert to keep breathing gas temperature at a comfortable level; spare oxygen cylinder and coolant canister; lens insert for clear, fog-free vision for 4 h; wiper option available; service kit with all required service tools, spares, and lubricants.

Testing Information
Contact the U.S. Army Asst. Program Manager Major Steve Bonk at 703–704–3590 for live agent test data.

Applicable Regulations
Not specified

Health Hazards
Not specified

Communications Interface Capability
Not specified

EOD Compatibility
Not specified

General
Name
ID# 9

Bullard CC20 Series Airline Respirator

Technology

Unique air delivery system: A unique neck cuff design helps maintain positive pressure inside the hood to aid in keeping contaminants out. As air enters the hood, the inner collar inflates, providing a snug, comfortable fit around the neck and continuous flow of air to the worker's breathing zone. CC20 respirators provide a significantly higher level of protection at a lower cost than cartridge respirators.

Stock Number

Five models designed to protect workers in diverse job applications

Protection Type

Respiratory

Equipment Category

Respirator, airline
CC20 Series hood-style airline respirators consist of five Bullard components; all must be present and properly assembled to constitute a NIOSH-approved respirator. (Approval No. TC–19C–154, Type C).
1. Respirator hood.
2. Headband or head protection.
3. Breathing tube.
4. Flow control device.
5. Breathing air supply hose.

Availability

Not specified

Current User(s)

Manufacturing, pharmaceuticals, and painting

Manufacturer

Bullard
1898 Safety Way
Cynthiana, KY 41031–9303
800–827–0423 (Tel)
606–234–6611 (Tel)
606–234–6858 (Fax)

Manufacturer Type

Domestic

Developer

Bullard

Source

www.bullard.com
POC: Brian Shockley, Market Manager Occupational Health
859–234–6616, ext. 153 (Tel)
859–234–8987 (Fax)

Certification

MSHA/NIOSH for use in Type C applications. Permeation Guide contains permeation data for over 800 chemicals based on the ASTM F739, TC–19C–154, Type C.

Operational Parameters
Chemical Warfare (CW)
Agents Protected Against

Not specified

Biological Warfare (BW) Agents Protected Against	Not specified
Toxic Industrial Materials (TIMs) Protected Against	Warning: CC20 respirators are not approved for use in any atmosphere immediately dangerous to life or health (IDLH) or from which the wearer cannot escape without the use of a respirator. Permeation Guide contains permeation data for over 800 chemicals based on the ASTM F739. Tychem QC and Tychem SL provide splash and liquid penetration protection against many chemicals. Refer to DuPont Permeation Guide for fabric details.
Duration of Protection	The Dupont Permeation Guide contains permeation data for over 800 chemicals based on the ASTM F739 test method for resistance of protective clothing materials to permeation by liquid or gases under conditions of continuous contact.
Recommended Use(s)	Chemical and pesticide handling, pharmaceutical manufacturing, nuclear facilities, spray painting and coating operations.

Physical Parameters

Sizes Available	Not specified
Weight	Not specified
Package Size and Volume	Not specified
Power Requirements	Not specified
Material Type	For increased protection in chemical and pharmaceutical applications, two special models are available. The SICN model is constructed from Tyvek®/Saranex® 23P and the TICSN model is fabricated from Tyvek® QC. Both feature an outer bib covering the shoulders and extending to the waist with side fasteners to keep the bib secured during work operations. Tychem QC and Tychem SL provide splash and liquid penetration protection against many chemicals. Refer to DuPont Permeation Guide for fabric details.
Construction Type	Patented neck cuff inflates for comfortable, dependable seal. Taped seams on both models provide added protection against liquid penetration.
Color	White

Logistical Parameters

Ease of Use	The CC20 hood is lighter and more comfortable than tight fitting facemasks. It covers the entire head, face, and neck - providing splash/overspray protection and making cleanup quick and easy. The CC20 hood does not require fit testing and elaborate record keeping. It also easily accommodates beards, prescription eyewear, or safety glasses.
Consumables	Not specified
Maintenance Requirements	Inexpensive enough to be disposable; durable enough for reuse
Shelf Life	Inexpensive enough to be disposable; durable enough for reuse
Transportability	Not specified
Operational Limitations	A variety of optional climate control devices helps increase productivity by allowing workers to cool or warm incoming air to meet individual comfort requirements
Environmental Conditions	Not specified
Unit Cost	Not specified
Maintenance Cost	Not specified
Warranty	Not specified
Don/Doff Information	Not specified
Use/Reuse	CC20 respirator hoods are durable enough to reuse, yet inexpensive enough to discard after each use, depending on the work application.

Launderability	Not specified
Accessories	Not specified
Special Requirements	
Training Requirements	Not specified
Training Available	Not specified
Manuals Available	Not specified
Surveillance Testing Requirements	Not specified
Support Equipment	Not specified
Testing Information	Not specified
Applicable Regulations	Not specified
Health Hazards	Not specified
Communications Interface Capability	Not specified
EOD Compatibility	Not specified

General

Name
ID# 10

Bullard Spectrum-PDE Pressure Demand Respirator with ESCBA

Technology

Continuous flow; respirator with Escape Air cylinder; Spectrum PDE Combination PD/5 min or 10 min ESCBA for confined spaces and hazardous work environments. Strong, durable harness and waist belt are fire retardant.

Stock Number

Not supplied

Protection Type

Respiratory

Equipment Category

Respirator; escape air cylinder (PD or ESCBA). Respirator operates efficiently with compressed or bottled air as the air source, improving worker mobility. Strong, durable harness and waist belt are fire retardant, providing the worker with an added measure of security on the job. Regulator hose is routed securely over the shoulder, enhancing comfort and safety. Approved with eight quick-disconnect coupler assemblies, providing compatibility with most workplace breathing air systems.

Availability

Commercial

Current User(s)

Manufacturing, painting, and rescuing

Manufacturer

Bullard
1898 Safety Way
Cynthiana, KY 41031–9303
800–827–0423 (Tel)
606–234–6611 (Tel)
606–234–6858 (Fax)

Manufacturer Type

Domestic

Developer

Bullard

Source

www.bullard.com
POC: Brian Shockley, Market Manager Occupational Health
859–234–6616, ext. 153 (Tel)
859–234–8987 (Fax)

Certification

TC–19C–322, TC–19C–354, TC–13F–387, TC–13F–388, and TC–19C–321

Operational Parameters

Chemical Warfare (CW) Agents Protected Against

Not specified

Biological Warfare (BW) Agents Protected Against

Not specified

Toxic Industrial Materials (TIMs) Protected Against

Not specified

Duration of Protection	Not specified
Recommended Use(s)	For confined and hazardous atmospheres including those which are IDLH. For spray painting and general industrial use.

Physical Parameters

Sizes Available	Small, medium, and large
Weight	Not specified
Package Size and Volume	Not specified
Power Requirements	Not specified
Material Type	Standard harness is made from fire retardant nylon. A benefit for those customers who are using the product in environments where there is potential for flashover.
Construction Type	Not specified
Color	Black

Logistical Parameters

Ease of Use	Padded shoulder harness is easily adjustable for a comfortable, balanced cylinder. Regulator hose positions securely over the shoulder, keeping close to the worker's body during operations in tight spaces.
Consumables	Not specified
Maintenance Requirements	Not specified
Shelf Life	Not specified
Transportability	Not specified
Operational Limitations	Compatible with a variety of optional climate control assemblies
Environmental Conditions	Not specified
Unit Cost	Not specified
Maintenance Cost	Not specified
Warranty	Not specified
Don/Doff Information	Pressure demand versions feature a "first breath" feature, which permits donning of the respirator without free flow, conserving the air supply
Use/Reuse	Not specified
Launderability	Not specified
Accessories	Regulator with bypass that allows adjustable, continuous flowing air to the worker for comfort and/or defogging the lens, when necessary

Special Requirements

Training Requirements	Not specified
Training Available	Not specified
Manuals Available	Not specified
Surveillance Testing Requirements	Not specified
Support Equipment	Not specified
Testing Information	Not specified
Applicable Regulations	Not specified
Health Hazards	Not specified
Communications Interface Capability	Not specified
EOD Compatibility	Not specified

General
Name
ID# 11

Sabre Tornado® Respiratory System (Airline)

Technology | Constant flow airline respirator
Stock Number | T-A-Line
Protection Type | Respiratory
Equipment Category | Airline: The Tornado airline (T-A-Line) is designed for use with compressed airline sources and also for use with the full range of six Tornado headtops, offering maximum operational flexibility. The unit includes a built-in filter that acts as a silencer to minimize airflow noise and increase wearer comfort. It also acts as a secondary filter that visually signals the user if the air supply contains oil.

Availability | Not specified
Current User(s) | Industrial and manufacturing
Manufacturer | Bullard
1898 Safety Way
Cynthiana, KY 41031-9303
800-827-0423 (Tel)
606-234-6611 (Tel)
606-234-6858 (Fax)

Manufacturer Type | Domestic
Developer | Bullard Sabre LLC.
Source | www.bullard.com
POC: Brian Shockley, Market Manager Occupational Health
859-234-6616, ext. 153 (Tel)
859-234-8987 (Fax)
Certification | Not specified

Operational Parameters
Chemical Warfare (CW) Agents Protected Against | Not specified
Biological Warfare (BW) Agents Protected Against | Not specified
Toxic Industrial Materials (TIMs) Protected Against | Not specified
Duration of Protection | Not specified
Recommended Use(s) | Painting and general industrial use

General

Physical Parameters

Sizes Available	Sizes available to fit all head types
Weight	Not specified
Package Size and Volume	Not specified
Power Requirements	Not specified
Material Type	Not specified
Construction Type	Not specified
Color	Not specified

Logistical Parameters

Ease of Use	Easily converts to Powered air purifying respirator (PAPR)
Consumables	Not specified
Maintenance Requirements	Not specified
Shelf Life	Not specified
Transportability	Not specified
Operational Limitations	The unit includes a built-in filter that acts as a silencer to minimize airflow noise and increase wearer comfort.
Environmental Conditions	Not specified
Unit Cost	Not specified
Maintenance Cost	Not specified
Warranty	Not specified
Don/Doff Information	Not specified
Use/Reuse	Not specified
Launderability	Not specified
Accessories	Not specified

Special Requirements

Training Requirements	Not specified
Training Available	Not specified
Manuals Available	Not specified
Surveillance Testing Requirements	Not specified
Support Equipment	Not specified
Testing Information	Not specified
Applicable Regulations	Not specified
Health Hazards	Not specified
Communications Interface Capability	Not specified
EOD Compatibility	Not specified

General
Name
ID# 12

Sabre Tornado® Respiratory System (PAPR)

Technology	Powered Air-Purifying Respirator (PAPR)
Stock Number	T-Power
Protection Type	Respiratory
Equipment Category	PAPR: The Tornado (T-Power) unit is designed to provide filtered air for the widest range of industrial applications. Other safety features include a battery lock to prevent accidental disconnection and a special on/off switch that requires positive action to turn the unit off.
Availability	Not specified
Current User(s)	Not specified
Manufacturer	Bullard
	1898 Safety Way
	Cynthiana, KY 41031-9303
	800-827-0423 (Tel)
	606-234-6611 (Tel)
	606-234-6858 (Fax)
Manufacturer Type	Domestic
Developer	Bullard Sabre LLC.
Source	www.bullard.com
	POC: Brian Shockley, Market Manager Occupational Health
	859-234-6616, ext. 153 (Tel)
	859-234-8987 (Fax)
Certification	T-Power units are certified to NIOSH regulations 42 CFR 84

Operational Parameters

Chemical Warfare (CW) Agents Protected Against	Not specified
Biological Warfare (BW) Agents Protected Against	Not specified
Toxic Industrial Materials (TIMs) Protected Against	Not specified
Duration of Protection	Not specified
Recommended Use(s)	Laboratories, pharmaceuticals, agriculture, chemicals, and general industrial

Physical Parameters

Sizes Available	Not specified
Weight	Not specified
Package Size and Volume	Not specified
Power Requirements	Not specified

Material Type	Not specified
Construction Type	Not specified
Color	Not specified
Logistical Parameters	
Ease of Use	Easily converts to airline use
Consumables	Not specified
Maintenance Requirements	The unit is also designed to require no routine maintenance and is tamper resistant. Establish filter change-out schedule specific to your application. Visit www.bullard.com for assistance.
Shelf Life	Not specified
Transportability	Not specified
Operational Limitations	Not specified
Environmental Conditions	Not specified
Unit Cost	Not specified
Maintenance Cost	Not specified
Warranty	Not specified
Don/Doff Information	Not specified
Use/Reuse	Not specified
Launderability	Not specified
Accessories	Not specified
Special Requirements	
Training Requirements	Not specified
Training Available	Not specified
Manuals Available	Not specified
Surveillance Testing Requirements	
Support Equipment	Not specified
Testing Information	Not specified
Applicable Regulations	Not specified
Health Hazards	Not specified
Communications Interface Capability	Not specified
EOD Compatibility	Not specified

General

Name   *SR-100, 60 Minute ESCBA*

ID# 13

Picture Not Available

Technology

Chemical based rebreather (KO_2/LiOH). The unit uses a bi-directional rebreathing system in which exhaled gas makes two passes through a CO_2 absorption/oxygen generation canister before the breathing gas is inhaled by the user. Specific amounts of potassium super-oxide (KO_2) and lithium hydroxide (LiOH) are used to produce O_2 and scrub CO_2, respectively, resulting in the production of a minimum of 100 L of O_2.

Stock Number   Q152000006

Protection Type   Respiratory

Equipment Category   ESCBA, escape only

Availability   Commercial

Current User(s)   Not specified

Manufacturer
CSE Corporation
600 Seco Road
Monroeville, PA 15146
800–245–2224 (Tel)
412–856–9203 (Fax)
customerservice@csecorporation.com

Manufacturer Type   Domestic

Developer   CSE with cooperation of MSHA

Source
jgt@csecorporation.com
POC: Mr. Tocci

Certification
NIOSH/MSHA Certification under TC–13F–239. Designed to meet CFR 30, part 75–1714 and CFR 29, 1910,146 Appendix E.

Operational Parameters

Chemical Warfare (CW) Agents Protected Against   Not specified

Biological Warfare (BW) Agents Protected Against   Not specified

Toxic Industrial Materials (TIMs) Protected Against
Protection of workers in confined spaces against toxic gases, oxygen deficiency, and smoke inhalation.

Duration of Protection
Rated Duration: 60 min (minimum) depending on the user's physical work rate. Deliverable O_2: 3.5 ft^3/100 L.

Recommended Use(s)
Confined spaces such as manholes, sewers, vaults, tanks, vessels, tunnels, silos, mines, wet wells, waste water, clean rooms, semiconductor labs, and submarines.

Physical Parameters

Sizes Available
Choice of six belt sizes:
Small (28 in to 34 in) to XX-large (51 in to 57 in)
Accessory belt sizes: S, M, L, XL, XXL, and XXXL

Weight
Weight carried: 5.7 lb
Weight in use: 4.9 lb

Package Size and Volume   7–3/4 in x 4 in x 5–1/2 in

Power Requirements   Battery pack

Material Type	Nylon accessory belt, durable nylon carrying pouch, suspenders, Velcro strap, and reflective strips.
Construction Type	Double stitched nylon and Velcro strap
Color	Not specified

Logistical Parameters

Ease of Use	Belts sized for perfect fit, load-supporting suspenders
Consumables	Not specified
Maintenance Requirements	Not specified
Shelf Life	10 yr; storage conditions 32 °F to 130 °F
Transportability	Designed to be worn on a belt
Operational Limitations	Not specified
Environmental Conditions	All common outdoor weather conditions
Unit Cost	$550 per unit Accessories are extra cost
Maintenance Cost	Not specified
Warranty	1 yr
Don/Doff Information	By following the steps written by MSHA/NIOSH, the unit can be donned in less than 20 s when worn on the worker's belt.
Use/Reuse	Yes, by following readiness check
Launderability	Nylon belt and suspenders can be laundered
Accessories	Each unit is supplied complete with a starter oxygen cylinder, goggles, case, and approved pouch. Optional reflective belts, suspenders, and pouches are available.

Special Requirements

Training Requirements	Training unit, training video
Training Available	Training video
Manuals Available	Training video
Surveillance Testing Requirements	Can be checked instantly by visually inspecting the moisture indicators in the top and bottom covers. The indicators are blue as long as seals are intact. If the seal has been broken, and moisture has contaminated the unit, the moisture indicators will turn pink or white .
Support Equipment	Carrying pouch, suspenders, belt, battery pouch, training video, user manual, acoustics solids movement detector, ASMD spot checker, acoustics solids movement detector kit, and storage box.
Testing Information	Not specified
Applicable Regulations	Not specified
Health Hazards	Not specified
Communications Interface Capability	Not specified
EOD Compatibility	Not specified

General

Name
ID# 14

AirBoss PSS100 with Flashing Gauge or with Sentinel

Technology

AirBoss PSS100 is designed to shift the weight of the unit from the shoulders to the hips, reducing back strain and increasing stability. The Draeger SCBA utilizes the same pneumatics and technology advanced components found on the AirBoss Evolution unit.

Stock Number
Not specified

Protection Type
Respiratory

Equipment Category
SCBA

Availability
Commercially

Current User(s)
- Miami Dade Fire Department (FL)
  305-361-1066/305-596-8634 (Tel)
- Kennet Square Fire Co. (PA)
  215-444-8410 (Tel)
- Lester Fire Co. (PA)
  610-521-3944 (Tel)
- Thorndale Fire Co. (PA)
  610-383-4835 (Tel)
- Lower Providence Township (PA)
  610-539-6560 (Tel)

Manufacturer
Draeger Safety, Inc.
101 Technology Drive
Pittsburgh, PA 15275

Manufacturer Type
Domestic/Foreign

Developer
Draeger Limited
Kitty Brewster Industrial Estate
Blyth, Northumberland, United Kingdom NE24 4RG
011-44-167-035-2891 (Tel)

Source
Draeger Safety, Inc.
POC: Julie Malinowski
412-787-8383 (Tel)
800-922-5518 (Tel)
412-787-2207 (Fax)

Certification
NIOSH and MSHA; NFPA compliant to standard 1981/1997 edition;
IPASS II or Sentinel compliant to 1982/1998 edition.

Operational Parameters

Chemical Warfare (CW)
Agents Protected Against
All (agents not specified)

Biological Warfare (BW) Agents Protected Against	All (agents not specified)
Toxic Industrial Materials (TIMs) Protected Against	All (not specified)
Duration of Protection	30 min, 45 min, or 60 min, dependent on the type of cylinder selected. AirBoss Sentinel calculates air supply time based upon actual usage and first warns when 50 % of air is used.
Recommended Use(s)	First responders

Physical Parameters

Sizes Available	One size fits all masks
Weight	Dependent on the type of cylinder selected (from 20 lb to 30 lb with cylinder)
Package Size and Volume	PSS100: 28.5 L in x 11 W in x 7 H in
Power Requirements	For Flashing Gauge: 2 N cell batteries. For Super IPASS II and AirBoss Sentinel: 9 V battery. Recommend yearly battery charge for all.
Material Type	Lightweight carbon composite backplate; mask available in EPDM and silicone; Kevlar/Nomex harness is fire retardant and passes NFPA flame tests.
Construction Type	Two-piece construction facilitates vertical movement without over-balancing; preformed waist; entire weight of unit carried on hips, not shoulders; sliding point on waistbelt allows stretch and return movement when bending; shoulder straps always properly aligned.
Color	Black/blue

Logistical Parameters

Ease of Use	Two-piece construction facilitates vertical movement without over-balancing; all units with standard comfort pad and quick release coupling; 90 % peripheral vision. The unit is also designed to move with the wearer, both horizontally and vertically. This additional flexibility allows the wearer to work more effectively for longer periods of time, with less fatigue. The revolutionary adjustable 3 position backplate gives the wearer a means to achieve the perfect fit for any torso length.
Consumables	Air for cylinders
Maintenance Requirements	Recommended yearly: Flow and static test, replace ball nose o-ring, check medium pressure. Monthly: Check cylinder pressure. After use: visual inspection, functional and leak test, charge cylinder to correct pressure.
Shelf Life	Lifetime for aluminum cylinders and 15 yr for composite cylinders
Transportability	Easily transported
Operational Limitations	Not specified
Environmental Conditions	Designed to function under extremely harsh conditions; -32 °F to 160 °F NFPA—1981 Flame test (2000 °F for 10 s)
Unit Cost	$2K to $4.6K (depending on unit and options)
Maintenance Cost	Each year: $1.65 for Ball nose o-ring
Warranty	5/15 limited (5 yr bumper to bumper) (15 yr pressure reducer)
Don/Doff Information	None required
Use/Reuse	Reusable

Launderability	Clean/disinfect mask and Lung Demand Valve with AirKem 33. Harness can be laundered.
Accessories	For Flashing Gauge: IPASS On all units: Buddy breather, ChargAir, comfort pad, quick release is optional; auxiliary airline connection; medium pressure connection extension hose and pouch; pressure reducer; radio interface, hair net (NFPA compliant), soft carrying bag, and rapid adaptor.

Special Requirements

Training Requirements	3 h of training required
Training Available	Operational Level I and Maintenance Level II
Manuals Available	Information for use, service manual
Surveillance Testing Requirements	See maintenance requirements
Support Equipment	Streamlined nonaspirating whistle integrated into gauge assembly
Testing Information	Fit Test Reports, Field of View
Applicable Regulations	NIOSH, MSHA, and NFPA
Health Hazards	Not specified
Communications Interface Capability	Radio interface and voice amplification
EOD Compatibility	Not specified

General
Name
ID# 15

AirBoss Evolution with Flashing Gauge or with Sentinel

Technology
This NIOSH certified SCBA often exceeds the standard requirements of NIOSH and NFPA, and offers not only high performance, but reliability, durability, and comfort.

Stock Number
Not specified

Protection Type
Respiratory

Equipment Category
SCBA: The AirBoss Evolution is designed especially for use in professional fire fighting applications. With many options and accessories available, the AirBoss can be tailor-fit to meet specific needs.

Availability
Commercially available

Current User(s)
Memphis Fire Dept, Pittsburgh Bureau of Fire, Miami Fire Department, American River (CA), Mexican Navy, Bayer Fire Department (MO), Puerto Rico Fire Department, Western Taney County (MO), Berkeley Fire Department, Celanese, FMC Corporation Grand Junction Fire Department, Lyndon Fire and Rescue (KY), Nevada County (CA), Cal Energy (CA), Park City Fire Department (UT), Western Kentucky Gas (KY), Humane Fire Department (PA), and Bellagio Hotel (NV), to name several.

Manufacturer
Draeger Safety, Inc.
101 Technology Drive
Pittsburgh, PA 15275

Manufacturer Type
Domestic/Foreign

Developer
Draeger Limited
Kitty Brewster Industrial Estate
Blyth, Northumberland, United Kingdom NE24 4RG
011–44–167–035–2891 (Tel)

Source
Draeger Safety, Inc.
POC: Julie Malinowski
412–787–8383 (Tel)
800–922–5518 (Tel)
412–787–2207 (Fax)

Certification
NIOSH/MSHA
NFPA compliant to standard 1981/1997 edition
IPASS II or Sentinel compliant to 1982/1998 edition

Operational Parameters
Chemical Warfare (CW) Agents Protected Against
All (agents not specified)

Biological Warfare (BW) Agents Protected Against
All (agents not specified)

Toxic Industrial Materials (TIMs) Protected Against
All (not specified)

Duration of Protection	30 min, 45 min, or 60 min, dependent on the type of cylinder selected
Recommended Use(s)	First responders
Physical Parameters	
Sizes Available	Not specified
Weight	Dependent on the type of cylinder selected (from 20 lb to 30 lb with cylinder)
Package Size and Volume	24.5 L in x 12.5 W in x 6 H in
Power Requirements	For Flashing Gauge: 2 N cell batteries For Super IPASS II and AirBoss Sentinel: 9 V battery Recommend yearly battery charge for all
Material Type	Carbon composite backplate is light and maintains its ergonomic shape throughout the life of the product; Kevlar/Nomex harness is fire retardant and passes NFPA flame tests; and optional padding.
Construction Type	Not specified
Color	Black/blue
Logistical Parameters	
Ease of Use	Universal cylinder strap accommodates all cylinder configurations. Quick release coupling available on second stage regulator line; and 90 % peripheral vision.
Consumables	Air for cylinders
Maintenance Requirements	Recommended yearly: flow and static test, replace ball nose o-ring, replace sintered filter, check medium pressure. Monthly: check cylinder pressure. After use: visual inspection, functional and leak test, and charge cylinder to correct pressure.
Shelf Life	Lifetime for aluminum cylinders and 15 yr for composite cylinders
Transportability	Easily transported
Operational Limitations	Not specified
Environmental Conditions	Designed to function under extremely harsh conditions; -32 °F to 160 °F NFPA—1981 Flame test (2000 °F for 10 s)
Unit Cost	$2K to $4.6K (depending on unit and options)
Maintenance Cost	Each year: $1.65 for ball nose o-ring
Warranty	5/15 limited (5 yr bumper to bumper) (15 yr pressure reducer)
Don/Doff Information	None required
Use/Reuse	Reusable
Launderability	Clean/disinfect mask and Lung Demand Valve with AirKem 33. Harness can be laundered.
Accessories	For Flashing Gauge: IPASS On all units: Buddy breather, ChargAir, comfort pad, quick release is optional; universal cylinder strap accommodates all cylinder configurations; optional high pressure cylinder filling line; auxiliary airline connection, medium pressure connection extension hose and pouch, radio interface, hair net (NFPA compliant), soft carrying bag, and rapid adaptor
Special Requirements	
Training Requirements	3 h of training required
Training Available	Operational Level I and Maintenance Level II
Manuals Available	Information for use and service manual
Surveillance Testing Requirements	See maintenance requirements
Support Equipment	Streamlined nonaspirating whistle integrated into gauge assembly. Whistle sounds in excess of 90 dBA upon activation.

Testing Information   Fit Test Reports and Field of View

Applicable Regulations   NIOSH and NFPA

Health Hazards   Not specified

Communications Interface Capability   Radio interface and voice amplification

EOD Compatibility   Not specified

<u>*General*</u>
Name
ID# 16

BG-4 w/Mask

Technology	BG-4 w/Mask, cylinder and valve, single use canister and metal case
Stock Number	4055888
Protection Type	Respiratory
Equipment Category	Respirator, supplied air
Availability	Commercially available (4 wk delivery time)

Current User(s)	• Consolidation Coal Company
	  724–966–3441 (Tel)
	• Twenty Mile Coal Company
	  970–870–2735 (Tel)
	• Kentucky Department of Mines and Minerals
	  502–573–0140 (Tel)
	• Federal Bureau of Investigation (FBI)
	• City of Chicago Fire Department
	  312–747–7234 (Tel)

Manufacturer	Draeger Safety, Inc. 101 Technology Drive Pittsburgh, PA 15275
Manufacturer Type	Domestic/Foreign
Developer	Draeger Sicherheitstechnik GmbH Revalstrabe 1 Germany 23560 011–49–451–882–2000 (Tel)
Source	Draeger Safety, Inc. POC: Julie Malinowski 412–787–8383 (Tel) 800–922–5518 (Tel) 412–787–2207 (Fax)
Certification	NIOSH and MSHA

<u>*Operational Parameters*</u>

Chemical Warfare (CW) Agents Protected Against	Not specified
Biological Warfare (BW) Agents Protected Against	Not specified
Toxic Industrial Materials (TIMs) Protected Against	Not specified
Duration of Protection	4 h
Recommended Use(s)	Not specified

Physical Parameters

Sizes Available	Not specified
Weight	33 lb
Package Size and Volume	23.35 in x 18 in x 7.3 in
Power Requirements	9 V battery (4 h to 6 h of operation)
Material Type	Not specified
Construction Type	Not specified
Color	Not specified

Logistical Parameters

Ease of Use	Not specified
Consumables	Soda-lime, filters, and oxygen
Maintenance Requirements	Minimal
Shelf Life	Not specified
Transportability	Not specified
Operational Limitations	Not specified
Environmental Conditions	23 °F to 86 °F (operating temperature) 23 °F to 77 °F @ 30 % to 70 % relative humidity (storage temperature)
Unit Cost	Not specified
Maintenance Cost	Not specified
Warranty	1 yr
Don/Doff Information	None required
Use/Reuse	Reusable
Launderability	Not specified
Accessories	Not specified

Special Requirements

Training Requirements	8 h to 10 h of training required
Training Available	Yes
Manuals Available	User manual
Surveillance Testing Requirements	RZ test after each use
Support Equipment	None
Testing Information	No information available
Applicable Regulations	Not specified
Health Hazards	Not specified
Communications Interface Capability	Not specified
EOD Compatibility	Not specified

Name   *ProAir Evolution*
ID# 17

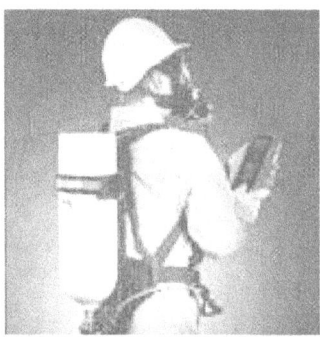

Technology   High performance industrial breathing apparatus. Positive pressure activated upon first breath.

Stock Number   Not specified

Protection Type   Respiratory

Equipment Category   SCBA, positive pressure activated upon first breath. Can be customized to meet specific needs.

Availability   Commercially available

Current User(s)
- Wackenhut Security Services (SC)
- Lifeguard H2S Safety Services (Tyler, TX)
  903–561–7506 (Tel)
- ParaSafe (Overton, TX)
  903–895–4462 (Tel)
- Aldrich Chemicsl (Milwaukee, WI)
  414–273–3850 (Tel)
- Ben and Jerry's
  802–752–1380 (Tel)

Manufacturer   Draeger Safety, Inc.
101 Technology Drive
Pittsburgh, PA 15275

Manufacturer Type   Domestic/Foreign

Developer   Draeger Ltd.
Kitty Brewster Industrial Estate
Blyth, Northumberland, United Kingdom NE24 4RG
011–44–167–035–2891 (Tel)

Source   Draeger Brochure
Draeger Safety, Inc.
POC: Julie Malinowski
412–787–8383 (Tel)
800–922–5518 (Tel)
412–787–2207 (Fax)

Certification   NIOSH

Operational Parameters

Chemical Warfare (CW) Agents Protected Against   All

Biological Warfare (BW) Agents Protected Against   All

Toxic Industrial Materials (TIMs) Protected Against   All

Duration of Protection	30 min, 45 min,and 60 min
Recommended Use(s)	Industrial environments

Physical Parameters

Sizes Available	One size fits all masks
Weight	Depends on cylinder selected. All under 31 lb.
Package Size and Volume	24.5 in x 12.5 in x 6.4 in
Power Requirements	None required
Material Type	Carbon composite backplate is light and maintains its ergonomic shape throughout the life of the product; nylon harness and carbon composite backplate.
Construction Type	Direct cylinder connection to pressure reducer removes dangers of exposed and unrestricted high pressure hoses
Color	Black

Logistical Parameters

Ease of Use	Universal cylinder strap accommodates all cylinder configurations; easy to use after initial training; and 90 % peripheral vision.
Consumables	Air for cylinders
Maintenance Requirements	Yearly: flow and static test, replace ball nose o-ring, check medium pressure. Monthly: check cylinder pressure. After use: visual inspection, functional and leak test, and charge cylinder to correct pressure.
Shelf Life	Lifetime for aluminum cylinders and 15 yr for composite cylinders
Transportability	Easily transported
Operational Limitations	Not specified
Environmental Conditions	Designed to function under extremely harsh conditions; -32 °F to 160 °F
Unit Cost	$1K to $2K depending on unit and options
Maintenance Cost	Each Year: $1.65 for ball nose o-ring
Warranty	5 yr bumper to bumper; 15 yr on the first stage reducer
Don/Doff Information	None required
Use/Reuse	Reusable
Launderability	Clean/disinfect mask and Lung Demand valve with AirKem 33. Harness can be laundered. No limit to either.
Accessories	Flashing gauge, IPASS, buddy breather, ChargAir, comfort pad, quick release are optional; pressure reducer guaranteed 100 % fail-safe. No need for redundant or second pressure reducer.

Special Requirements

Training Requirements	3 h of training required
Training Available	Operational Level I and Maintenance Level II
Manuals Available	Information for use and service manual
Surveillance Testing Requirements	See maintenance requirements
Support Equipment	Streamlined nonaspirating whistle integrated into gauge assembly. Whistle sounds in excess of 90 dBA upon activation
Testing Information	Fit Test Reports and Field of View
Applicable Regulations	NIOSH

Health Hazards   Not applicable
Communications Interface   Radio interface and voice amplification
Capability
EOD Compatibility   Not specified

General

Name
ID# 18

Panorama Nova Full Facepiece

Technology	Negative pressure full-face mask
Stock Number	EPDM—R51525
	Silicone—R51535
Protection Type	Respiratory
Equipment Category	Respirator and negative pressure
Availability	Commercially available
Current User(s)	Westinghouse Savannah River Site
Manufacturer	Draeger Safety, Inc.
	101 Technology Drive
	Pittsburgh, PA 15275
Manufacturer Type	Domestic/Foreign
Developer	Draeger Sicherheitstechnik GmbH
	Revalstrabe 1
	Germany 23560
	011−49−451−882−2000 (Tel)
Source	Draeger Safety, Inc.
	POC: Julie Malinowski
	412−787−8383 (Tel)
	800−922−5518 (Tel)
	412−787−2207 (Fax)
Certification	NIOSH, NFPA

Operational Parameters

Chemical Warfare (CW) Agents Protected Against	Nerve, blister and blood agents: GA, GB, GD, VX, HD, and L
Biological Warfare (BW) Agents Protected Against	With P100 cartridges, becomes 99.97 % efficient
Toxic Industrial Materials (TIMs) Protected Against	Various
Duration of Protection	Dependent on filter used
Recommended Use(s)	Not specified

Physical Parameters

Sizes Available	One size fits all (smallest female to largest male)
Weight	1.3 lb (21 oz)
Package Size and Volume	1 ft^3
Power Requirements	None
Material Type	EPDM (ethylene propylene dimonomer) or silicone; Plexiglas lens; stainless steel speech diaphragm

Construction Type	Triple sealing edge assures firm and comfortable fit
Color	Black for EPDM, yellow for silicone

Logistical Parameters

Ease of Use	Very easy to use. Range of movement maintained, and maximum vision maintained.
Consumables	Wide range of NIOSH-approved single screw-in cartridges
Maintenance Requirements	Replace valves every 2 yr. Wash and disinfect as required.
Shelf Life	Not specified
Transportability	Very transportable
Operational Limitations	Not specified
Environmental Conditions	Designed to function under extremely harsh conditions
Unit Cost	$153 to $192
Maintenance Cost	$2/yr
Warranty	1 yr
Don/Doff Information	None required
Use/Reuse	Reusable
Launderability	Recommend use of AirKem 33A for washing/disinfecting with no limitations
Accessories	Spectacle kits, easy donning headstraps, communication devices are optional accessories

Special Requirements

Training Requirements	Less than 5 min
Training Available	Maintenance/testing training available
Manuals Available	User manual
Surveillance Testing Requirements	Not specified
Support Equipment	None
Testing Information	NIOSH test data is available
Applicable Regulations	OSHA
Health Hazards	None
Communications Interface Capability	BaComm Voice Amplification Unit (attaches to mask, no tools required, and radio connections also available)
EOD Compatibility	Not specified

General

Name
ID# 19

Paret Defend Air

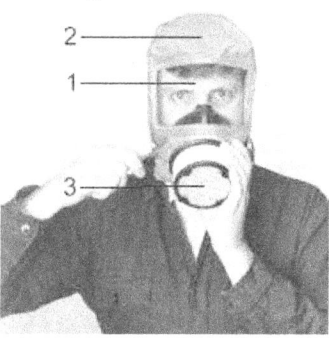

Technology	Escape hood, not powered
Stock Number	R54797—Paret DE
	R51906—Wall Mount Bracket
Protection Type	Respiratory
Equipment Category	Escape hood and not powered
Availability	Commercially available
Current User(s)	Not specified
Manufacturer	Draeger Safety, Inc.
	101 Technology Drive
	Pittsburgh, PA 15275
Manufacturer Type	Domestic/Foreign
Developer	Draeger Sicherheitstechnik GmbH
	Revalstrabe 1
	Germany 23560
	011–49–451–882–2000 (Tel)
Source	Draeger Safety, Inc.
	POC: Julie Malinowski
	412–787–8383 (Tel)
	800–922–5518 (Tel)
	412–787–2207 (Fax)
Certification	Not specified

Operational Parameters

Chemical Warfare (CW) Agents Protected Against	Nerve and blister
Biological Warfare (BW) Agents Protected Against	Not specified; P100 filter is attached which is 99.97% efficient
Toxic Industrial Materials (TIMs) Protected Against	Arsine, chlorine, hydrogen cyanide, and phosgene
Duration of Protection	20 min of vapor protection and 20 min of permeation resistance
Recommended Use(s)	First responders, law enforcement or emergency response personnel

Physical Parameters

Sizes Available	One size fits all (smallest female to largest male)
Weight	30 oz (packaged in hard plastic case) and 1.3 lb (22 oz) unpackaged
Package Size and Volume	7.5 in x 5.3 in x 3.1 in (l x h x w) packaged
Power Requirements	None
Material Type	Coated Tyvek; flame retardant self extinguishing PVC; lens treated with anti-mist agent

Construction Type	Sealed seams (neckseal to provide 1000 PF)
Color	Gray

Logistical Parameters

Ease of Use	Very easy to use. Range of movement maintained, 80 % of natural field of vision retained.
Consumables	None
Maintenance Requirements	Replace valves every 2 yr. Wash and disinfect as required.
Shelf Life	5 yr in original packaging. Storage temperature not to exceed 158 °F.
Transportability	Very transportable
Operational Limitations	No restrictions
Environmental Conditions	Designed to function under extremely harsh conditions
Unit Cost	$125
Maintenance Cost	None
Warranty	1 yr
Don/Doff Information	Less than 10 s
Use/Reuse	Disposable
Launderability	None
Accessories	Wall mount bracket is available

Special Requirements

Training Requirements	Less than 5 min
Training Available	Not specified
Manuals Available	User manual
Surveillance Testing Requirements	Not specified
Support Equipment	Not specified
Testing Information	Extensive testing such as shock and vibration, package impact tests, visor fogging tests, and low temperature tests (according to confidential draft)
Applicable Regulations	Not specified
Health Hazards	Disposal of used equipment varies based on local regulations
Communications Interface Capability	Not necessary since there are no mouthbits or nose clips. With an integrated half mask, the wearer can speak normally.
EOD Compatibility	Not specified

General

Name *Kareta M Mask*
ID# 20

Picture Not Available

Technology	Dual eyepiece mask
Stock Number	Not specified
Protection Type	Respiratory
Equipment Category	Respirator and dual eyepiece mask
Availability	Commercially available
Current User(s)	Not specified
Manufacturer	Draeger Safety, Inc.
	101 Technology Drive
	Pittsburgh, PA 15275
Manufacturer Type	Domestic/Foreign
Developer	Draeger Sicherheitstechnik GmbH
	Revalstrabe 1
	Germany 23560
	011–49–451–882–2000 (Tel)
Source	Draeger Brochure
	Draeger Safety, Inc.
	POC: Julie Malinowski
	412–787–8383 (Tel)
	800–922–5518 (Tel)
	412–787–2207 (Fax)
Certification	NIOSH

Operational Parameters

Chemical Warfare (CW) Agents Protected Against	Not specified
Biological Warfare (BW) Agents Protected Against	Not specified
Toxic Industrial Materials (TIMs) Protected Against	Not specified
Duration of Protection	Not specified
Recommended Use(s)	First responders

Physical Parameters

Sizes Available	Not specified
Weight	Not specified
Package Size and Volume	Not specified
Power Requirements	None
Material Type	Not specified
Construction Type	Not specified
Color	Black

Logistical Parameters

Ease of Use	Not specified
Consumables	Accepts all Draeger NIOSH-approved cartridges
Maintenance Requirements	Not specified

Shelf Life	Not specified
Transportability	Not specified
Operational Limitations	Not specified
Environmental Conditions	Not specified
Unit Cost	Not specified
Maintenance Cost	Not specified
Warranty	Not specified
Don/Doff Information	Not specified
Use/Reuse	Not specified
Launderability	Not specified
Accessories	Drinking device connection included

Special Requirements

Training Requirements	Not specified
Training Available	Not specified
Manuals Available	Not specified
Surveillance Testing Requirements	Not specified
Support Equipment	Not specified
Testing Information	Not specified
Applicable Regulations	NIOSH
Health Hazards	Not specified
Communications Interface Capability	MegaComm Voice Amplification Unit (attaches to mask, no tools required, and radio connections also available)
EOD Compatibility	Not specified

General

Name
ID# 21

Duram Emergency Escape Respirator

Picture Not Available

Technology

The emergency escape respirator provides short-term (5 min to 15 min) respiratory protection against chemical and/or biological warfare agents and common industrial chemicals through its outstanding filtering and fit properties. This product provides integrated protection.

Stock Number

DM–54C–600V–YE/BE

Protection Type

Respirator

Equipment Category

Emergency escape respirator for use in the event of a toxic release of chemical or biological agents

Availability

Average shipment 4 wk

Current User(s)

Los Angeles City HAZMAT Department L.A. County HAZMAT Department, U.S. Marines HRT Team, Federal Bureau of Investigation, Georgia Fire Department, St. Louis Fire Department, Conoco Oil Company, McDonald Douglas, and Emerson Electric.

Manufacturer

Duram Rubber Products
Kibbutz Ramat Hakovesh, Israel, 44930
U.S. Distributor:
POC: Herbert D. Rassbach
Wayne, PA 19087
610–964–8555 (Tel)
610–975–9185 (Fax)
hdrassbach@hdrgroup.com
POC: John J. Schramko
Westminster, MA 01473
978–874–0214 (Tel)
978–876–5878 (Fax)
jschr40499@aol.com

Manufacturer Type

Foreign

Developer

Duram Rubber Products, Kibbutz Ramat Hakovesh, Israel, 44930

Source

WMD Protective Systems, Inc. were invited to present the Duram Emergency Escape Mask to both the Personal Protective and Operational Equipment, and Medical sub groups of the recently convened Marshall Convention, (Standardized Weapons of Mass Destruction Response Force Equipment and interoperability) November 2–4, 1999.

Certification

Recognized U.S. Standards do not exist for negative pressure air purifying escape respirators. Testing of the Duram Emergency Escape Respiratory has been performed at Edgewood Research Development and Engineering Center, U.S. Army Chemical and Biological Defense Command.

Operational Parameters

Chemical Warfare (CW) Agents Protected Against

Short-term protection against volatile agents such as cyanogen chloride (CK), and semi-volatile agents such as mustard and the G-agents. Concentration (mg/m^3), break through time (min), flow rate (L/min). Cyanogen chloride (CK) 250 mg/m^3, 15 min, 30 L/min. Dimethylmethylft phosphonate (DMMP) 1000 mg/m^3, 5 min, 30 L/min.

Biological Warfare (BW) Agents Protected Against

The Duram Emergency Escape Respirator provides protection against biological agents as evidenced by Oil and NaCl (salt) aerosol tests.

Toxic Industrial Materials (TIMs) Protected Against	Provides protection against vapors with a boiling point higher than 65 °C, certain inorganic gases and vapors, ann other acidic gases and vapors. High Hazard TIMs: Carbon tetra-chloride (CCl_4), hydrogen cyanide (HCN), chlorine (Cl_2), hydrogen sulphide (H_2S), sulfur dioxide (SO_2), and ammonia (NH_3). Tested against a wide range of police chemical weapons including: Pyro CS, Pyro CN, Smoke, OC spray, OC foam, CS spray, CN spray, ClearOut Gas (OC+CN), CS dust and CN dust. These tests were conducted in fully enclosed or semi-enclosed areas with chemical concentrations many times greater than normal. The spray and foam tests were performed at close range (3 ft to 4 ft) using long bursts (2 s to 4 s) directly on the visor and filter sections of the respirator.
Duration of Protection	The Duram Emergency Escape Respirator is a single use product for short duration exposure to chemical/biological warfare agents, toxic industrial materials and police chemical weapons.
Recommended Use(s)	The Duram Emergency Escape Respirator is designed to provide emergency escape respiratory protection for egress from a incident involving chemical /biological warfare agents, toxic industrial materials and police chemical suppression agents. The suggested uses are for individuals exposed to these environments. The product is appropriate for both emergency personnel, which would include Fire (HAZMAT), Structural Fire Fighters, Police, EMT's, Hospital personnel, and individuals exposed to the hazards described above in the event of a terrorist incident involving Weapons of Mass Destruction (WMD).

Physical Parameters

Sizes Available	One size fits all. This provides for ease of issuing and low inventory costs.
Weight	110 g
Package Size and Volume	18 cm x 14 cm x 1.5 cm
Power Requirements	Not applicable
Material Type	Hood is constructed of polychloroprene, visor is constructed of polyimide (DuPont Kapton 100 HN), filter is a multiple construction consisting of electrostatic particulate filter with activated charcoal filter layers.
Construction Type	Hood and visor are heat-sealed. Filter assembly is installed with adhesives. Exhalation valve is a mechanical seal.
Color	Yellow

Logistical Parameters

Ease of Use	The Duram Emergency Escape Respirator is a single use one size fits all mask. In over 125 wear tests the respirator was easily and quickly donned by expert and inexperienced users. The respirator can be used by individuals with long hair and facial hair as well as eyeglass wearers.
Consumables	Not applicable. The respirator is a single use disposable product.
Maintenance Requirements	Not applicable
Shelf Life	5 yr from manufacturing date
Transportability	A packaged mask can be carried in the pocket of a coat or worn on a belt
Operational Limitations	The Duram Emergency Escape Respirator visor received the highest UL–94 flammability rating; V–O. The Duram Emergency Escape Respirator hood passed the rigorous requirements of NFPA 701, 1972 edition.
Environmental Conditions	Store in an environment protected from extreme heat and humidity. It is supplied in an airtight vacuum package. In a test conducted at Edgewood Arsenal, the respirators were stored for a 12 wk period at 71 °C.

Inspection of the masks after the test duration found the packages intact and the product useable for its intended purpose.

Unit Cost	$70 to $90 per unit depending on quantity
Maintenance Cost	Not applicable.
Warranty	In general the respirator is warranted to be free from defects in material and workmanship and effective for a period of 5 yr
Don/Doff Information	No assistance is required to don or doff the respirator
Use/Reuse	Not applicable, the respirator is a single use devise
Launderability	Not applicable, the respirator is a single use devise
Accessories	Not applicable, the respirator is single use with no replaceable components

Special Requirements

Training Requirements	The Duram Emergency Escape Respirator is a simple devise which needs no training to use
Training Available	Not applicable
Manuals Available	Use instructions are printed on the vacuum package
Surveillance Testing Requirements	Simply insure that the vacuum package is intact
Support Equipment	Not applicable
Testing Information	Protection factors: the Duram Emergency Escape Respirator has been tested for the qualification of fit factors from the 5 % army female to the 95 % army male by Edgewood Research Development and Engineering Center, U.S. Army Chemical and Biological Defense Command. This achieved a protection factor of 549 compared to the U.S. Army Expedient Hood with a Protection factor of 416.
Applicable Regulations	There are no consensus standards for Air Purifying Emergency Escape Respirators. NIOSH does not have a category for nonpowered air purifying escape masks or negative pressure masks that employ a neck seal.
Health Hazards	None
Communications Interface Capability	Not applicable. The Duram Emergency Escape Respirator offers excellent verbal communication ability especially when compared to tight fitting air purifying respirators.
EOD Compatibility	Not specified

General

Name
ID# 22

PP mask with ABP3/US canister

Technology   Positive Pressure in PAPR System; could be used as negative pressure

Stock Number   Without canister:
Size: XL—105 93 942
Size: L—105 93 944
Size: M—105 93 945
Size: S—105 93 946

Protection Type   Respiratory

Equipment Category Mask/positive pressure in PAPR system. Mask/negative pressure stand alone.

Availability   Commercially available

Current User(s)   French Army (gas mask), French Civil Defense, Hungarian Army (gas mask), Polish Army (gas mask)

Manufacturer   GIAT Industries 13, route de la Minière
78034 Versailles Cedex, France
33 (1) 30 97 39 91 (Tel)
33 (1) 30 97 39 67 (Fax)
http://www.giat-industries.fr

Manufacturer Type   Foreign

Developer   GIAT Industries

Source   GIAT Industries
North American Distributor:
The CENTECH GROUP, Inc
4600 North Fairfax Drive, Suite 400
Arlington, VA 22203
800–938–1026 (Tel)
703–525–2349 (Fax)
www.centechgroup.com

Certification   Positive pressure: NIOSH-approved (French version EN approved)
Negative pressure: EN approved in French version

Operational Parameters

Chemical Warfare (CW) Agents Protected Against   All NATO CW threats at NATO standard

Biological Warfare (BW) Agents Protected Against   Yes, Hepa P3 canister in accordance with NATO threat

Toxic Industrial Materials (TIMs) Protected Against   Yes—NIOSH standard for NH_3, CL_2, CCl_4, HCN, ammonia, and chlorine
No—carbon monoxide (CO)

Duration of Protection   Liquid proof 24 h against G and H agents ($10g/m^2$)

Recommended Use(s)   Tactical operation and crisis management (8 h)

Physical Parameters

Sizes Available	4 sizes: S, M, L, and XL
Weight	1.2 lb (mask only) and 1.4 lb (with canister)
Package Size and Volume	11 in x 9 in x 7 in (mask only)
Power Requirements	None
Material Type	The mask is constructed of polyurethane material (impermeable); canister (plastic case, active carbon, and paper)
Construction Type	Full face respirator
Color	Black

Logistical Parameters

Ease of Use	Compatible with a wide range of personal protective equipment
Consumables	ABP3/US canister
Maintenance Requirements	Exchange the canister every 5 yr. Cleaning and checking of expiration valve every 5 yr in PAPR. Cleaning and checking of expiration valve every 1 yr in negative pressure use.
Shelf Life	5 yr without maintenance
Transportability	No restriction known
Operational Limitations	Military standard
Environmental Conditions	Military standard
Unit Cost	On request
Maintenance Cost	Low cost
Warranty	1 yr
Don/Doff Information	None required
Use/Reuse	Decontamination and or sanitary cleaning
Launderability	Laundered using cleaning kit. Decontamination not applicable by boiling.
Accessories	Optical device, harness, and transportation bag

Special Requirements

Training Requirements	Less than 1 h of training is required
Training Available	On request
Manuals Available	Illustrated user manual
Surveillance Testing Requirements	Fit test once a year
Support Equipment	Standard means
Testing Information	EN certificate number: NIOSH certificate: TC–23C–2041; French Army Test Report for mask
Applicable Regulations	NIOSH
Health Hazards	Not Known
Communications Interface Capability	Not specified
EOD Compatibility	Compatible with GIAT catalog suits (TOMPS, SWAT, and Level C)

Name PAPR system

ID# 23

PAPR system

Technology
PAPR system with PP (positive pressure) mask, ABP3/US canister, CASU (blower)

Stock Number
Kit of 4 pieces:
Size: L and M—106 16 414
Size: S and XL—106 22 737

Protection Type
Respiratory

Equipment Category
PAPR/positive pressure

Availability
Commercially available

Current User(s)
French Army (gas mask), French Civil Defense, Hungarian Army (gas mask), Polish Army (gas mask)

Manufacturer
GIAT Industries 13, route de la Minière
78034 Versailles Cedex, France
33 (1) 30 97 39 91 (Tel)
33 (1) 30 97 39 67 (Fax)
http://www.giat-industries.fr

Manufacturer Type
Foreign

Developer
GIAT Industries

Source
GIAT Industries
North American Distributor:
The CENTECH GROUP, Inc
4600 North Fairfax Drive, Suite 400
Arlington, VA 22203
800–938–1026 (Tel)
703–525–2349 (Fax)
www.centechgroup.com

Certification
NIOSH-approved (French version EN approved)

Operational Parameters

Chemical Warfare (CW) Agents Protected Against
All NATO CW threats at NATO standard

Biological Warfare (BW) Agents Protected Against
Yes, HEPA P3 canister on accordance with NATO threat

Toxic Industrial Materials (TIMs) Protected Against
Yes—NIOSH standard for NH_3, CL_2, CCl_4, HCN, ammonia, and chlorine
No—carbon monoxide (CO)

Duration of Protection
Liquid proof, 24 h against G and H agents ($10g/m^2$)

Recommended Use(s)
Tactical operation and crisis management (8 h)

Physical Parameters

Sizes Available	4 sizes: S, M, L, and XL
Weight	55 lb for kit for 4 responders
	6.6 kg (1 set without package)
Package Size and Volume	Kit for 4 responders: 18 in x 31 in x 15.7 in
Power Requirements	One lithium battery for use and one as a spare part in the package
Material Type	The mask is constructed of polyurethane material (impermeable); canister (plastic case, active carbon, and paper); blower (plastic case, and electric engine)
Construction Type	Full face respirator
Color	Black

Logistical Parameters

Ease of Use	Compatible with a wide range of personal protective equipment
Consumables	ABP3/US canister; lithium battery
Maintenance Requirements	Exchange the canister every 5 yr; cleaning and checking of expiration valve every 5 yr; exchange gastight female threaded connector every 5 yr; exchange Lithium battery every 10 yr
Shelf Life	5 yr without maintenance
Transportability	No restriction known
Operational Limitations	Military standard
Environmental Conditions	Military standard
Unit Cost	On request
Maintenance Cost	Low cost
Warranty	1 yr
Don/Doff Information	None required
Use/Reuse	Decontamination and or sanitary cleaning
Launderability	Laundered using cleaning kit. Decontamination not applicable by boiling.
Accessories	Optical device

Special Requirements

Training Requirements	Less than 1 h of training is required
Training Available	On request
Manuals Available	Illustrated user manual
Surveillance Testing Requirements	Fit test once a year
Support Equipment	Standard means
Testing Information	EN certificate number: NIOSH certificate: TC-23C-2041; French Army Test Report for mask
Applicable Regulations	NIOSH
Health Hazards	Not Known
Communications Interface Capability	Not specified
EOD Compatibility	Compatible with GIAT catalog suits (TOMPS, SWAT, and Level C)

General
Name
ID# 24

EVATOX Adult Escape Hood US

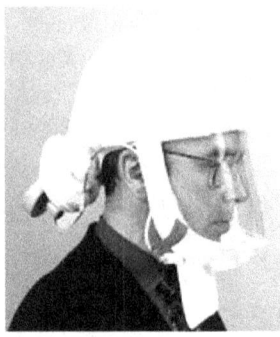

Technology   Escape hood powered with canister type A1B1E1K1P3
Stock Number   106 03 922
Protection Type   Respiratory
Equipment Category   Escape hood powered
Availability   Commercially available
Current User(s)   French civil defense, French Fire Brigades
Manufacturer   GIAT Industries 13, route de la Minière
                          78034 Versailles Cedex, France
                          33 (1) 30 97 39 91 (Tel)
                          33 (1) 30 97 39 67 (Fax)
                          http://www.giat-industries.fr

Manufacturer Type   Foreign
Developer   GIAT Industries
Source   GIAT Industries
                          North American Distributor:
                          The CENTECH GROUP, Inc
                          4600 North Fairfax Drive, Suite 400
                          Arlington, VA 22203
                          800-938-1026 (Tel)
                          703-525-2349 (Fax)
                          www.centechgroup.com
Certification   EN in progress

Operational Parameters
Chemical Warfare (CW) Agents Protected Against   No

Biological Warfare (BW) Agents Protected Against   Yes. Hepa P3 canister on accordance with NATO threat.

Toxic Industrial Materials (TIMs) Protected Against Organic vapors are covered with GIAT cartridges, no carbon monoxide. EN standard covering ammonia and organic vapors.

Duration of Protection   > 4 h of wearing (battery)
Recommended Use(s)   Escape for adults

Physical Parameters
Sizes Available   1 size fits all
Weight   36 oz
Package Size and Volume   24 in x 14 in x 6 in
Power Requirements   2 x 1.5 V batteries provided

Material Type	Hood: PE (polyethylene), PU (polyuren) , PVC; canister (aluminum, active carbon, and paper); blower (electric engine, plastic, and alkaline batteries)
Construction Type	Powered hood (built in blower) 2 cfm
Color	Yellow

Logistical Parameters

Ease of Use	Easy donning compatible with standard spectacles and with beards
Consumables	None
Maintenance Requirements	Change battery and canister every 3 yr
Shelf Life	9 yr (with maintenance every 3 yr)
Transportability	No restriction known
Operational Limitations	Rugged for emergency use
Environmental Conditions	As canistered equipment: minimum oxygen 17 % and no CO presence
Unit Cost	On request
Maintenance Cost	Low cost
Warranty	1 yr
Don/Doff Information	Very easy, no assistance
Use/Reuse	Single use
Launderability	No decon, disposable after exposure
Accessories	None

Special Requirements

Training Requirements	2 h for rescuers
Training Available	On request
Manuals Available	Supplied with equipment
Surveillance Testing Requirements	Every 3 yr change battery and canisters
Support Equipment	Standard means
Testing Information	Manufacturer test
Applicable Regulations	F0531 105 21 085
Health Hazards	Not Known
Communications Interface Capability	Not specified
EOD Compatibility	With every suit

General

Name
ID# 25

M40 Series Gas Mask

Technology
Respirator/canister. Component(s): canister, canister mount, drinking device, exhalation valve, eyepiece(s), facepiece, head harness, inhalation valve, nosecup, and facepiece of molded silicone rubber. Two eyepieces are made of CR39 and held in place by metal eyerings. The internal nosecup is made of silicone rubber. Canister is attached directly to the mask. Hood composed of butyl-coated nylon and EPDM rubber for use in a chemically contaminated environment.

Stock Number
Small: 4240-01-258-0061
Medium: 4240-01-258-0062
Large: 4240-01-258-0063

Protection Type
Respiratory

Equipment Category
Respirator/canister

Availability
Note: To order Hycar M40 series masks, contact MSA International (412-967-3483) Military

Current User(s)
Infantry and civilian surety workers. Used by U.S. Army and Marine Corps. Also used in a special purpose mode by EOD.

Manufacturer
ILC Dover, Inc.
P.O. Box 266
Harrington Road
Frederica, DE 19946
302-335-3911 (Tel)
302-335-0762 (Fax)

Mine Safety Appliances Co.
Defense Products Department
P.O. Box 428
Pittsburgh, PA 15230
412-733-9270 (Tel)
412-733-8573 (Fax)

Manufacturer Type
Domestic

Developer
U.S. Army Chemical Research, Development, and Engineering Center
Edgewood Area
Aberdeen Proving Ground, MD 21010-5423

Source
Worldwide NBC Mask Handbook

Certification
Canister Mount—NATO Standard

Operational Parameters

Chemical Warfare (CW) Agents Protected Against
Provides protection of the eyes and respiratory system against chemical agents. Worn with a hood in chemically contaminated environment.

Biological Warfare (BW) Agents Protected Against
Provides protection of the eyes and respiratory system against biological agents

Toxic Industrial Materials (TIMs) Protected Against	Not intended to provide protection against carbon monoxide or ammonia
Duration of Protection	Greater than 330000 mg-min/m^3 for nerve agents and mustard
Recommended Use(s)	Infantry and civilian surety workers. Also used in a special purpose mode by EOD.

Physical Parameters

Sizes Available	Small, medium, and large
Weight	28 oz (facepiece and canister) 10 oz (canister) 18 oz (facepiece)
Package Size and Volume	Not specified
Power Requirements	Not specified
Material Type	Facepiece of molded silicone rubber. Two eyepieces are made of CR39 and held in place by metal eyerings. The internal nosecup is made of silicone rubber. Canister is attached directly to the mask. Hood composed of butyl-coated nylon and EPDM rubber for use in a chemically contaminated environment.
Construction Type	Canister is attached directly to the mask
Color	Black

Logistical Parameters

Ease of Use	Mask has six-point adjustable head harness. Several preplanned improvements to be incorporated into the series design including improved vision correction, ballistic and laser eye protection, a quick-doff hood/second skin, interchangeable microphone system, voice amplification unit, and canister interoperability system.
Consumables	C2 canister or any other NATO standard thread canister
Maintenance Requirements	Not specified
Shelf Life	Not determined
Transportability	Not specified
Operational Limitations	Not specified
Environmental Conditions	Not specified
Unit Cost	$150
Maintenance Cost	Not specified
Warranty	Not specified
Don/Doff Information	Less than 9 s
Use/Reuse	Not specified
Launderability	Not specified
Accessories	Includes carrier, hood, 2 clear outserts, 2 tinted outserts, and second skin

Special Requirements

Training Requirements	Not specified
Training Available	Not specified
Manuals Available	Not specified
Surveillance Testing Requirements	Not specified
Support Equipment	Hood to be used in chemically contaminated environment
Testing Information	Meets AR 70–71 requirements for decontamination. M258A1 Skin Decon Kit is stored in the carrier. M258A1 is being replaced with M291 and will not be stored in the carrier.

Applicable Regulations	Not specified
Health Hazards	Not specified
Communications Interface Capability	Accessories include the ESP Communications System. Voicemitters are located on the front and side of the mask.
EOD Compatibility	Can be used in a special purpose mode by EOD

Name
ID# 26

M42 Series Gas Mask

Technology

Respirator/canister. Component(s): canister, canister mount, drinking device, exhalation valve, eyepiece(s), facepiece, head harness, inhalation valve, and nosecup. Facepiece of molded silicone rubber. Two eyepieces are made of CR39 and held in place by metal eyerings. The internal nosecup is made of silicone rubber. Canister is attached directly to the mask. Hood composed of butyl-coated nylon and EPDM rubber for use in a chemically contaminated environment.

Stock Number

Small: 4240-01-258-0064
Medium: 4240-01-258-0065
Large: 4240-01-258-0066

Protection Type

Respiratory

Equipment Category

Respirator/canister

Availability

Military

Current User(s)

Military combat vehicle crews (U.S. Army and Marine Corps). Also used in a special purpose mode by EOD.

Manufacturer

ILC Dover, Inc.
P.O. Box 266
Harrington Road
Frederica, DE 19946
302-335-3911 (Tel)
302-335-0762 (Fax)

Mine Safety Appliances Co.
Defense Products Department
P.O. Box 428
Pittsburgh, PA 15230
412-733-9270 (Tel)
412-733-8573 (Fax)

Manufacturer Type

Domestic

Developer

U.S. Army Chemical Research, Development, and Engineering Center
Edgewood Area
Aberdeen Proving Ground, MD 21010-5423

Source

Worldwide NBC Mask Handbook

Certification

Canister Mount—NATO Standard

Operational Parameters

Chemical Warfare (CW)
Agents Protected Against

Provides protection of the eyes and respiratory system against chemical agents. Worn with a hood in chemically contaminated environment.

Biological Warfare (BW)
Agents Protected Against

Provides protection of the eyes and respiratory system against biological agents

Toxic Industrial Materials (TIMs) Protected Against	Not intended to provide protection against carbon monoxide or ammonia
Duration of Protection	Greater than 330000 mg-min/m^3 for nerve agents and mustard
Recommended Use(s)	Combat vehicle crews. Also used in a special purpose mode by EOD.

Physical Parameters

Sizes Available	Small, medium, and large
Weight	36 oz (facepiece and canister) 10 oz (canister) 26 oz (facepiece)
Package Size and Volume	Not specified
Power Requirements	Not specified
Material Type	Facepiece of molded silicone rubber. Two eyepieces are made of CR39 and held in place by metal eyerings. The internal nosecup is made of silicone rubber. Canister is attached directly to the mask. Hood composed of butyl-coated nylon and EPDM rubber for use in a chemically contaminated environment.
Construction Type	Canister attached to the mask via a corrugated hose, and the canister is housed in a specially designed canister carrier
Color	Black

Logistical Parameters

Ease of Use	Mask has six-point adjustable head harness. Several preplanned improvements to be incorporated into the series design including improved vision correction, ballistic and laser eye protection, a quick-doff hood/second skin, interchangeable microphone system, voice amplification unit, and canister interoperability system.
Consumables	C2 canister or any other NATO standard thread canister
Maintenance Requirements	Not specified
Shelf Life	Not determined
Transportability	Not specified
Operational Limitations	Not specified
Environmental Conditions	Not specified
Unit Cost	$250
Maintenance Cost	Not specified
Warranty	Not specified
Don/Doff Information	Less than 9 s
Use/Reuse	Not specified
Launderability	Not specified
Accessories	Includes carrier, hood assembly, corrugated canister hose assembly, 2 clear and 2 tinted outserts, and a second skin

Special Requirements

Training Requirements	Not specified
Training Available	Not specified
Manuals Available	Not specified
Surveillance Testing Requirements	Not specified
Support Equipment	Hood to be used in chemically contaminated environment

Testing Information	Meets AR 70–71 requirements for decontamination. M258A1 Skin Decon Kit is stored in the carrier. M258A1 is being replaced with M291 and will not be stored in the carrier.
Applicable Regulations	Not specified
Health Hazards	Not specified
Communications Interface Capability	Accessories include the ESP Communications System. Voicemitters are located on the front and side of the mask.
EOD Compatibility	Can be used in a special purpose mode by EOD

General
Name
ID# 27

ARAP/C and ARAP/E Airline Respirators

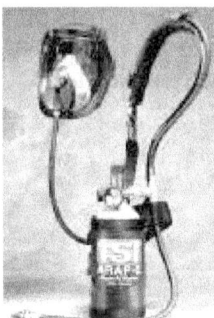

Technology

ARAP/C and ARAP/Escape provide the maximum respiratory protection in hazardous atmospheres. Designed to provide breathing air where ambient air may be irritating. The ARAP line is compatible with the Viking SCBA. It can be configured for use in airline and HAZMAT applications. ARAP/ESCAPE includes a 5 min, 10 min, or 15 min emergency escape cylinder that can be activated with a simple rotation of the cylinder valve. ARAP/ESCAPE can be worn in atmospheres that are considered immediately dangerous to life or health (IDLH).

Stock Number
Complete ARAP assembly: 707.135.00

Protection Type
Respiratory

Equipment Category
Respirator, compatible with SCBA or can be configured for use in airline applications

Availability
Commercial

Current User(s)
Not specified

Manufacturer
International Safety Instruments
922 Hurricane Shoals Road
Lawrenceville, GA 30243
770-962-2552 (Tel)
770-963-2797 (Fax)
Mary McDougald, Marketing Coordinator
Customer Service: 888-ISI-SAFE (Tel)

Manufacturer Type
Domestic and International

Developer
ISI

Source
www.intsafety.com
Mary McDougald, Marketing Coordinator
Customer Service: 888-ISI-SAFE (Tel)

Certification
NIOSH-approved Type C respirators

Operational Parameters
Chemical Warfare (CW) Agents Protected Against
Not specified

Biological Warfare (BW) Agents Protected Against
Not specified

Toxic Industrial Materials (TIMs) Protected Against
ARAP/ESCAPE can be worn in atmospheres that are considered IDLH

Duration of Protection
5 min, 10 min, or 15 min emergency escape cylinder

Recommended Use(s)
Military, government, confined space, mining, construction, chemical manufacturing, oil and petroleum processing, aviation and aerospace, and transportation

Physical Parameters

Sizes Available	Facemask—small, medium, and large
Weight	Lightweight and comfortable
Package Size and Volume	Not specified
Power Requirements	Not specified
Material Type	Kevlar harness options. AirSwitch™ facemask made from silicone or neoprene.
Construction Type	Reverted-edge ensures proper seal. Standard nosecup eliminates fogging.
Color	Not specified

Logistical Parameters

Ease of Use	Simple design makes standard service and repair easy for end-user. No bulky regulator on waistbelt.
Consumables	Not specified
Maintenance Requirements	Simple, low-cost maintenance
Shelf Life	Not specified
Transportability	Not specified
Operational Limitations	Not specified
Environmental Conditions	All common outdoor weather conditions
Unit Cost	Not specified
Maintenance Cost	Not specified
Warranty	Not specified
Don/Doff Information	Manual
Use/Reuse	Not specified
Launderability	Harnesses easily removed and cleaned. Facemask is fully submersible.
Accessories	Pigtail assembly, fittings, and optional welding mask attachment

Special Requirements

Training Requirements	Not specified
Training Available	Not specified
Manuals Available	Yes
Surveillance Testing Requirements	Not specified
Support Equipment	Supply hose
Testing Information	Not specified
Applicable Regulations	Not specified
Health Hazards	Not specified
Communications Interface Capability	Communications 1 radio interface fits any ISI Airswitch Facemask and is adaptable to all radio types
EOD Compatibility	No

General

Name

ID# 28

Viking Digital SCBA

Technology

SCBA; the Viking Digital provides maximum respiratory protection in IDLH atmospheres. It was designed with firefighters in mind, however it has applications in police and HAZMAT instances. It can be ordered with a 30 min, 45 min, or 60 min cylinder. This SCBA has many unique features including an in-mask light display providing the following information: cylinder pressure status, acknowledgement of radio transmission, and activation of the "end of service alarm." For police applications, the lights inside the inner nosecup make the Viking Digital very stealth. Radio interface with an in-mask microphone and a silent, low pressure lighted alarm that only the user can observe, provides the needed information without any noise. Sanitizing the facemask is simple because it is fully submersible for cleaning. The waterproof microphone attached inside the facemask reduces external noise while transmitting with the option for hands free radio transmission.

Stock Number

Not specified

Protection Type

Respiratory

Equipment Category

SCBA, can be ordered with a 30 min, 45 min, or 60 min cylinder

Availability

Commercial

Current User(s)

Fire fighters, HAZMAT teams, police departments

Manufacturer

International Safety Instruments
922 Hurricane Shoals Road
Lawrenceville, GA 30243
770-962-2552 (Tel)
770-963-2797 (Fax)
Mary McDougald, Marketing Coordinator
Customer Service: 888-ISI-SAFE (Tel)

Manufacturer Type

Domestic and International

Developer

ISI

Source

www.intsafety.com

Certification

NIOSH-approved

Operational Parameters

Chemical Warfare (CW) Agents Protected Against

None

Biological Warfare (BW) Agents Protected Against

None

Toxic Industrial Materials (TIMs) Protected Against

Protection against a variety of TIMs (IDLH atmospheres)

Duration of Protection	30 min, 45 min, or 60 min emergency escape cylinder
Recommended Use(s)	Military, government, and confined space

Physical Parameters

Sizes Available	Facemask—small, medium, and large
Weight	~ 20 lb
Package Size and Volume	Not specified
Power Requirements	8 AA batteries
Material Type	Kevlar harness, and AirSwitch™ facemask made from silicone or neoprene
Construction Type	Reverted-edge ensures proper seal
Color	Black with gray cylinder

Logistical Parameters

Ease of Use	Simple design makes standard service and repair easy for end-user
Consumables	Not specified
Maintenance Requirements	Simple, low-cost yearly maintenance
Shelf Life	Not specified
Transportability	Not specified
Operational Limitations	Not specified
Environmental Conditions	All indoor and outdoor weather
Unit Cost	Not specified
Maintenance Cost	Not specified
Warranty	15 yr
Don/Doff Information	Video available, simple and easy
Use/Reuse	Not specified
Launderability	Harness straps easily removable for cleaning. Facemask is fully submersible for easy and complete cleaning.
Accessories	Buddy breather attachment, radio interface, PASS option

Special Requirements

Training Requirements	Not specified
Training Available	Video as well as maintenance training
Manuals Available	Yes
Surveillance Testing Requirements	Inspect unit prior to use for wear and tear of unit
Support Equipment	Supply hose
Testing Information	Not specified
Applicable Regulations	Not specified
Health Hazards	Not specified
Communications Interface Capability	Radio interface is adaptable to all radio types
EOD Compatibility	Yes

General
Name
ID# 29

Interspiro Spiroscape Escape BA

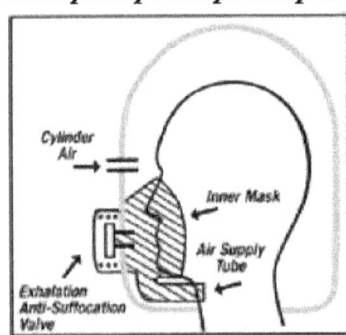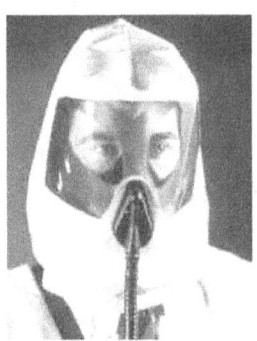

Technology

Spiroscape is the first emergency breathing apparatus to overcome the practical limitations of demand (unpredictable duration) and constant flow (CO_2 build up or heavy cylinder weight) type systems. Unique spiroscape air delivery system features an inner mask with exhalation valve and air supply tube. This allows CO_2 to be expelled from the hood optimizing the use of fresh air from the cylinder without the need for a demand valve. This unique constant flow system assures a predictable duration for air delivery. Patented auto hatch/safety valve automatically opens if air supply is exhausted to prevent employee suffocation. Can be used as standby fresh air hatch in staging areas. The auto hatch/safety valve also eliminates the need for a separate low air alarm system.

Stock Number

Spiroscape 10 or 15 min sets: P/N 95300
Auto fill adapter: P/N 95360
(EN or CGA connector and pressure to be specified)

Protection Type
Respiratory

Equipment Category
Escape breathing apparatus (for extreme emergency), constant flow

Availability
Available

Current User(s)
Not specified

Manufacturer
Interspiro Group
500 E. Main St.
Branford, CT. 06405
800–468–7788 (Tel)
203–481–3899 (Tel)
203–483–1879 (Fax)

Manufacturer Type
International

Developer
Interspiro

Source
www.interspiro.de
info@interspiro.com
Kenton D. Warner
203–483–8508 (Tel)

Certification
CE or NIOSH certification, cylinder size, and pressure to be specified

Operational Parameters

Chemical Warfare (CW)
Agents Protected Against
Not specified

Biological Warfare (BW)
Agents Protected Against
Not specified

Toxic Industrial Materials
(TIMs) Protected Against
Not specified

Duration of Protection	Predictable 10 min or 15 min duration options to cope with unexpected delays due to smoke, vapor clouds, complex escape routes, ladders, stairs, and employee apprehension
Recommended Use(s)	The traditional emergency escape breathing apparatus, is a basic emergency setup to help with evacuation in the unlikely event of a hazardous emergency

Physical Parameters

Sizes Available	Not applicable
Weight	Compact and lightweight
Package Size and Volume	Compact and lightweight
Power Requirements	Not applicable
Material Type	Rubber inner mask with exhalation valve; polyurethane coated high visibility outer hood; natural latex rubber neck seal, and wire reinforced air hose
Construction Type	Latex rubber neck provides superior fit and protection factors, eliminates draw string enclosures and elastic neck seals that stretch during washing or laundering
Color	Yellow

Logistical Parameters

Ease of Use	Quick start pull-tab guarantees automatic air activation prior to donning hood. Patented auto hatch/safety valve prevents suffocation when air supply is exhausted.
Consumables	Not specified
Maintenance Requirements	Unique anti-tamper tag verifies units integrity on inspection
Shelf Life	Not specified
Transportability	Light and transportable
Operational Limitations	10 min or 15 min
Environmental Conditions	Not specified
Unit Cost	Not specified
Maintenance Cost	Not specified
Warranty	Not specified
Don/Doff Information	No special instructions
Use/Reuse	Can be reused
Launderability	Can be laundered
Accessories	10 min or 15 min cylinders, wall mount, portable carrying case

Special Requirements

Training Requirements	Not specified
Training Available	Not specified
Manuals Available	Not specified
Surveillance Testing Requirements	Not specified
Support Equipment	Not specified
Testing Information	Not specified
Applicable Regulations	Not specified
Health Hazards	Unique patented auto hatch/safety valve automatically opens if air supply is exhausted to prevent employee suffocation. Can be used as standby

**Communications Interface
Capability**

fresh air hatch in staging areas. The auto hatch/safety valve also
eliminates the need for a separate low air alarm system

Not specified

EOD Compatibility

Not specified

General
Name — *Interspiro Respirator*
ID# 30

Picture Not Available

Technology — Respirator/Cartridge
Stock Number — Not specified
Protection Type — Respiratory
Equipment Category — Respirator/cartridge
Availability — Not specified
Current User(s) — Not specified
Manufacturer — Interspiro Group
500 E. Main St.
Branford, CT. 06405
Kenton D. Warner
203–483–8508 (Tel)
Manufacturer Type — Domestic
Developer — Not specified
Source — Lifecycle Plan SNL–795, September 30, 1998
Certification — Not specified

Operational Parameters
Chemical Warfare (CW) Agents Protected Against — Not specified
Biological Warfare (BW) Agents Protected Against — Not specified
Toxic Industrial Materials (TIMs) Protected Against — Not specified
Duration of Protection — Not specified
Recommended Use(s) — Not specified

Physical Parameters
Sizes Available — Not specified
Weight — Not specified
Package Size and Volume — Not specified
Power Requirements — Not specified
Material Type — Not specified
Construction Type — Not specified
Color — Not specified

Logistical Parameters
Ease of Use — Not specified
Consumables — C2A1
Maintenance Requirements — Not specified
Shelf Life — Not specified
Transportability — Not specified
Operational Limitations — Not specified
Environmental Conditions — Not specified
Unit Cost — Not specified

Maintenance Cost	Not specified
Warranty	Not specified
Don/Doff Information	Not specified
Use/Reuse	Not specified
Launderability	Not specified
Accessories	Not specified

Special Requirements

Training Requirements	Not specified
Training Available	Not specified
Manuals Available	Not specified
Surveillance Testing Requirements	Not specified
Support Equipment	Not specified
Testing Information	Not specified
Applicable Regulations	Not specified
Health Hazards	Not specified
Communications Interface Capability	Not specified
EOD Compatibility	Not specified

General

Name	*C4 Gas Mask*
ID# 31	
	Picture Not Available
Technology	Respirator
Stock Number	Black: 4240–21–908–1095
	Green: 4240–21–908–1096
	Tan: Available upon request
Protection Type	Respiratory
Equipment Category	Gas mask, respirator
Availability	Commercially available; immediate (green in production) black to special order
Current User(s)	Canadian Department of National Defense, Contact: DSSPM 2–8 (Royal Canadian Mounted Police and Denmark)
Manufacturer	Irvin Aerospace Canada Ltd.
	P.O. Box 280
	479 Central Avenue
	Fort Erie, Ontario L2A 5M9
	POC: Doug Eaton
	905–871–6510 (Tel)
	905–871–6534 (Fax)
	marketing@irvincanada.com
Manufacturer Type	Foreign
Developer	Canadian Department of National Defense
Source	Irvin Aerospace Canada Ltd.
	Rick Kosierb, MEng, CD
	NBC Program Manager
Certification	Canadian Department of National Defense

Operational Parameters

Chemical Warfare (CW) Agents Protected Against	All known military chemical agents
Biological Warfare (BW) Agents Protected Against	All known military biological agents
Toxic Industrial Materials (TIMs) Protected Against	Under study
Duration of Protection	24 h (in most cases)
Recommended Use(s)	Not specified

Physical Parameters

Sizes Available	XS, S, M, and L
Weight	16 oz without canister
Package Size and Volume	6 in x 8 in x 11 in
Power Requirements	Not applicable
Material Type	Bromobutyl rubber (impermeable)
Construction Type	Molded rubber
Color	Olive drab, optional black, and tan available upon request

Logistical Parameters

Ease of Use	Fast donning compatible with full protective gear
Consumables	Canister
Maintenance Requirements	Routine preventative maintenance
Shelf Life	10 yr minimum
Transportability	Fully transportable
Operational Limitations	Full military qualification
Environmental Conditions	All common military environmental conditions
Unit Cost	Volume dependent
Maintenance Cost	Not applicable
Warranty	1 yr
Don/Doff Information	None required
Use/Reuse	Can be reused
Launderability	Laundering: clean in water
	Decon: operator dependent
Accessories	Canister, carrier bag and communications, and gas mask cleaning system

Special Requirements

Training Requirements	1 h of training is required
Training Available	Operator and training course are available
Manuals Available	User, maintenance manual, and repair manual
Surveillance Testing Requirements	Routing leak testing is required
Support Equipment	None
Testing Information	Available from Irvin Aerospace Canada Ltd.
Applicable Regulations	None
Health Hazards	Used canister disposable as required
Communications Interface Capability	Not specified
EOD Compatibility	Not specified

General

Name
ID# 32

Litpac II-Rebreather

Picture Not Available

Technology

The LITPAC II is a closed circuit, 2 h, positive pressure self-contained breathing apparatus (SCBA). The unit can be worn in a Level A suit when circumstances dictate. Uses 38 % oxygen rather than more hazardous 100 % high-pressure oxygen. Inhalation temperatures are cooler than most other closed-circuit SCBAs.

Stock Number
4240–014526754

Protection Type
Respiratory

Equipment Category
SCBA, closed-circuit positive pressure

Availability
Commercially available since 1992

Current User(s)

- Contact: MGST Donald Holman
  MARCORSYSCOM Marine/NBC Program Management Office
  2033 Barnett Ave.
  Suite 315
  Quantico, VA 22134–5010
  703–784–5898 (Tel)
- Contact: Consequence Management Program Integration Office Dept. of Army
  Director of Military Support
  Attn: DAMO-ODC
  400 Army Pentagon
  Washington, D.C. 20310–0400
  703– 693–8983 (Tel)
- Contact: Captain Proctor
  City of St. Louis
  Fire Dept. Headquarters
  1421 N. Jefferson
  St. Louis, MO 63106
  314–533–1681 (Tel)
- Contact: Leonard Jufko
  Northeast Ohio Regional Sewer District
  4747 E. 49th Street
  Cleveland, OH 44125-1011
  216–641–6000 (Tel)
- Contact: Patricia Levenzon
  Impomak (for Minera Mechilla—Luis Andreani, Chief of Mining Operations)
  Emiliano Figueroa 839
  Santiago, Chili
  56–2–635–3188 (Tel)

Manufacturer
Litton Life Support
2734 Hickory Grove Road
P.O. Box 4508
Davenport, IA 52804
Contact: Dean Cantrill, Dir. of Commercial Products
319–383–6000 (Tel)
319–383–6125 (Fax)

Manufacturer Type
Domestic

Developer	Litton Life Support originally designed the LITPAC II to meet an Air Force requirement for a complete chemical and biological protection ensemble suitable for fire fighting. The original requirement was for 10000 SCBA with special design requirements for duration, profile, weight and breathing performance. Ten prototypes were built and sold to the Air Force for operational testing and evaluation. After assessing the results of the Air Force and in-house testing, many ergonomic improvements were incorporated into the unit. DOD funding for the LITPAC was canceled, but Litton Life Support decided to complete the development of the LITPAC II and to address the needs of this identified niche market.
Source	Litton Life Support: www.littonls.com
Certification	NIOSH/MSHA-approved, #TC–13F–233 for use in high radiant heat and open flame environments

Operational Parameters

Chemical Warfare (CW) Agents Protected Against	The unit can be worn in a Level A suit when circumstances dictate
Biological Warfare (BW) Agents Protected Against	The unit can be worn in a Level A suit when circumstances dictate
Toxic Industrial Materials (TIMs) Protected Against	The unit can be worn in a Level A suit when circumstances dictate
Duration of Protection	The LITPAC II is NIOSH rated as a 2 h device. The unit is designed to allow for rapid servicing with quick disconnects at all major attachment points. The soda lime and high pressure manifold assembly can be easily removed and replaced in the field if extended duration is required.
Recommended Use(s)	Not specified

Physical Parameters

Sizes Available	One size with adjustable straps on the head harness and shoulder harness
Weight	Slimline (just 4–3/8 in thick) and lightweight (30 lb)
Package Size and Volume	Slimline (just 4–3/8 in thick) and lightweight (30 lb)
Power Requirements	None
Material Type	Backpack housing—flame-retardant vinyl ester sheet molding compound Harnesses—Nomex, Kevlar, and flame-retardant polyurethane foam Buckles—(Item 1000–7101) polyetherimide resin Mask—silicone Mask adapter—polyphenylene sulfide Hoses—silicone
Construction Type	High pressure cylinder and rebreather mechanism enclosed in an unsealed case
Color	Safety yellow

Logistical Parameters

Ease of Use	The unit is compatible with all Level A and B response equipment (PPE), incorporates padded harnesses and flexible hoses, and has an "on demand" regulator allowing for easy breathing. The thickness of the unit is approximately 4–3/8 in and will allow a user to drive an unmodified truck, work in confined spaces or pass-through a standard manhole cover while wearing the unit. It provides freedom of motion in almost any situation and rides comfortably with the center of gravity within 1 in of geometric center of the unit. All control features are located for easy reach and manipulation.

Consumables	The soda lime and gas are consumed during operation. CO_2 scrubber and filters—(case of 12). Soda lime refill required after each complete 2 h usage of LITPAC II. O-Ring replacement as recommended by Maintenance Manuals. CO_2 scrubber (soda lime), O-Rings and filters—(case of 12). Soda lime refill required after each complete 2 h usage of LITPAC II. O-Ring replacement as recommended by maintenance manuals. The spare soda lime canister assembly (includes soda lime).
Maintenance Requirements	Level I—operator cleans, refills and leak checks after each use. Level 1 Maintenance Test Kit needed for pre and post usage of the LITPAC unit. Level II—annual diagnostic check.
Shelf Life	Shelf life of unit is indefinite Shelf life of components: bags—5 yr, pressure vessels—15 yr Shelf life of consumables: soda lime—2 yr, average
Transportability	The optional suitcase for the rebreather weighs 13.5 lb and can be hand carried. The quick-turn kit, including the suitcase, weighs 20 lb and can also be hand carried. The spare soda lime canister assembly, boxed, is 12 in x 7 in x 6 in and it weighs about 5 lb.
Operational Limitations	The unit has been fielded by the USMC CBIRF; the LITPAC II will function in weather conditions above -25 °F. It meets the NIOSH requirements for high-radiant heat and open flame environments. Inhalation temperatures cooler than most other closed-circuit SCBA's.
Environmental Conditions	The LITPAC II will function in weather conditions above -25 °F. It meets the NIOSH requirements for high-radiant heat and open flame environments.
Unit Cost	LITPAC II: $6.4K Carrying case: $246 Quick-turn kit: $3K Case of soda lime: $429 Soda lime canister: $114
Maintenance Cost	Maintenance on the LITPAC II is user performed. The Level 1 tester is $639 and the Level 2 tester is $7.9K
Warranty	Litton Life Support's standard terms and conditions include a 1 yr limited warranty
Don/Doff Information	No assistance is required.
Use/Reuse	The unit is reused; the soda lime is disposable
Launderability	Internal cleaning by user is a normal part of operations. It can be deconned as needed.
Accessories	No accessories are required for operational use. SCBA carrying case (recommended for storage and transportation). The spare pressure vessel assembly (complete with pressure vessel bag and carrying case). The spare soda lime canister assembly (includes soda lime). A manual is supplied with each unit.

Special Requirements

Training Requirements	1 h use instruction 5 h operations instruction (Level I) 20 h maintenance instruction (Level II)
Training Available	Level I and Level II training is available from Litton Life Support
Manuals Available	Instructions and Level I maintenance manual Level II maintenance manual

Surveillance Testing Requirements	Level I maintenance with Level I test kit
Support Equipment	No additional equipment is required to operate the primary unit; however, the user should establish a source for 38.5 % oxygen gas
Testing Information	NIOSH certification testing, and NIOSH comparative testing
Applicable Regulations	DOT regulations apply for transporting LITPAC II with full cylinders
Health Hazards	Not applicable as the expired soda lime is classified as a nonhazardous waste. An MSDS is available for the soda lime.
Communications Interface Capability	Not specified
EOD Compatibility	Not specified

General

Name
ID# 33

Easiflow Plus Full Facemask Respirator and Filters

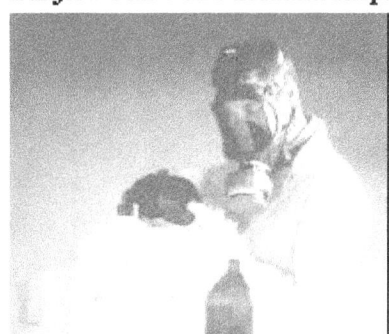

Technology

Negative pressure respirator; can be used in conjunction with Magnum P3 powered respiratory systems or fresh-air supply equipment. A lightweight, negative pressure full facemask designed for use in areas of toxic gases or highly toxic particles. Made from high quality silicone, the mask provides a high nominal protection factor of up to 2000 (dependent on filter used) due to the excellent seal around the face.

Stock Number
Not specified

Protection Type
Respiratory

Equipment Category
Respirator and negative pressure

Availability
Not specified

Current User(s)
Not specified

Manufacturer
Martindale Centurion Safety Products Ltd.
Howlett Way
Thetford, Norfolk, IP24 1HZ
England
+44 (0)1842 754266 (Tel)
+44 (0)1842 765590 (Fax)

Manufacturer Type
Foreign

Developer
Martindale Centurion Safety Products Ltd.

Source
Martindale Centurion Safety
www.centurionsafety.co.uk
sales@centurionsafety.co.uk
MPS Mine and Process Service Inc.
Box 484
Kewanee, IL 61443
309-852-6529 (Tel)
309-854-5206 (Fax)

Certification
CE certified by B.S.I. to EN136

Operational Parameters

**Chemical Warfare (CW)
Agents Protected Against**
Not applicable

**Biological Warfare (BW)
Agents Protected Against**
Not applicable

**Toxic Industrial Materials
(TIMs) Protected Against**
Will protect against TIMs of toxic dust when fitted with P3 filter

Duration of Protection
Up to 2 h

Recommended Use(s)
Not specified

Physical Parameters

Sizes Available	Not specified
Weight	Not specified
Package Size and Volume	Not specified
Power Requirements	Not specified
Material Type	Not specified
Construction Type	Not specified
Color	Not specified

Logistical Parameters

Ease of Use	Easily manageable, able to be worn for long periods with no effects
Consumables	Not specified
Maintenance Requirements	Not specified
Shelf Life	Not specified
Transportability	Not specified
Operational Limitations	Not limiting, has 75 % to 90 % visibility
Environmental Conditions	Protects in normal environments
Unit Cost	Less than or equal to $500 per unit
Maintenance Cost	Not specified
Warranty	Not specified
Don/Doff Information	Not specified
Use/Reuse	Able to be cleaned and reused greater than 50 times
Launderability	Not specified
Accessories	Not specified

Special Requirements

Training Requirements	Little to no training required
Training Available	Not specified
Manuals Available	Not specified
Surveillance Testing Requirements	Not specified
Support Equipment	Not specified
Testing Information	Not specified
Applicable Regulations	Not specified
Health Hazards	Not specified
Communications Interface Capability	Not specified
EOD Compatibility	Not specified

General

Name
ID# 34

Magnum 4000 P3, with Full Facemask

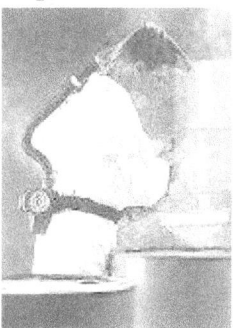

Technology	Powered respiratory system; uses internal cassette filter
Stock Number	TH3P/TM3P classification
Protection Type	Respiratory
Equipment Category	Respirator, powered
Availability	Not specified
Current User(s)	Not specified
Manufacturer	Martindale Centurion Safety Products Ltd.
	Howlett Way
	Thetford, Norfolk
	England IP24 1HZ
	+44 (0)1842 754266 (Tel)
	+44 (0)1842 765590 (Fax)
Manufacturer Type	Foreign
Developer	Martindale Centurion Safety Products Ltd.
Source	Martindale Centurion Safety
	www.centurionsafety.co.uk
	sales@centurionsafety.co.uk
	MPS Mine and Process Service Inc.
	Box 484
	Kewanee, IL 61443
	309-852-6529 (Tel)
	309-854-5206 (Fax)
Certification	CE certified by B.S.I. to EN12941 TH3P and EN 12942 TM3P

Operational Parameters

Chemical Warfare (CW) Agents Protected Against	Not applicable
Biological Warfare (BW) Agents Protected Against	Not applicable
Toxic Industrial Materials (TIMs) Protected Against	Will protect against TIMs of toxic dust when fitted with P3 filter
Duration of Protection	Up to 2 h
Recommended Use(s)	Not specified

Physical Parameters

Sizes Available	Not specified
Weight	Not specified
Package Size and Volume	Not specified
Power Requirements	Not specified

Material Type	Not specified
Construction Type	Not specified
Color	Not specified

Logistical Parameters

Ease of Use	Easily manageable, able to be worn for long periods with no effects
Consumables	Not specified
Maintenance Requirements	Not specified
Shelf Life	Not specified
Transportability	Not specified
Operational Limitations	Not limiting, has 75 % to 90 % visibility
Environmental Conditions	Protects in normal environments
Unit Cost	Less than or equal to $500 per unit
Maintenance Cost	Not specified
Warranty	Not specified
Don/Doff Information	Not specified
Use/Reuse	Able to be cleaned and reused greater than 50 times
Launderability	Not specified
Accessories	Not specified

Special Requirements

Training Requirements	Little to no training required
Training Available	Not specified
Manuals Available	Not specified
Surveillance Testing Requirements	Not specified
Support Equipment	Not specified
Testing Information	Not specified
Applicable Regulations	Not specified
Health Hazards	Not specified
Communications Interface Capability	Not specified
EOD Compatibility	Not specified

General

Name
ID# 35

Magnum 4500 P3, with Full Facemask

Technology

Powered respiratory system; fitted with DIN 40 thread for externally mounted screw threaded filter canister. Magnum 4500, P3 power unit for use with DIN 40 screw threaded filter canisters. TH3P/TM3P classification

Stock Number

Protection Type

Respiratory

Equipment Category

Respirator, powered

Availability

Not specified

Current User(s)

Not specified

Manufacturer

Martindale Centurion Safety Products Ltd.
Howlett Way
Thetford, Norfolk
England IP24 1HZ
+44 (0)1842 754266 (Tel)
+44 (0)1842 765590 (Fax)

Manufacturer Type

Not specified

Developer

Martindale Centurion Safety Products Ltd.

Source

Martindale Centurion Safety
www.centurionsafety.co.uk
sales@centurionsafety.co.uk
MPS Mine and Process Service Inc.
Box 484
Kewanee, IL 61443
309-852-6529 (Tel)
309-854-5206 (Fax)

Certification

CE certified by B.S.I. to EN12941 TH3P and EN 12942 TM3P

Operational Parameters

Chemical Warfare (CW) Agents Protected Against

Not applicable

Biological Warfare (BW) Agents Protected Against

Not applicable

Toxic Industrial Materials (TIMs) Protected Against

Will protect against TIMs of toxic dust when fitted with P3 filter

Duration of Protection

Up to 2 h

Recommended Use(s)

Not specified

Physical Parameters

Sizes Available

Not specified

Weight

Not specified

Package Size and Volume

Not specified

Power Requirements	Not specified
Material Type	Not specified
Construction Type	Not specified
Color	Not specified

Logistical Parameters

Ease of Use	Easily manageable, able to be worn for long periods with no effects
Consumables	Not specified
Maintenance Requirements	Not specified
Shelf Life	Not specified
Transportability	Not specified
Operational Limitations	Not limiting, has 75 % to 90 % visibility
Environmental Conditions	Protects in normal environments
Unit Cost	Less than or equal to $500 per unit
Maintenance Cost	Not specified
Warranty	Not specified
Don/Doff Information	Not specified
Use/Reuse	Able to be cleaned and reused greater than 50 times
Launderability	Not specified
Accessories	Not specified

Special Requirements

Training Requirements	Little to no training required
Training Available	Not specified
Manuals Available	Not specified
Surveillance Testing Requirements	Not specified
Support Equipment	Not specified
Testing Information	Not specified
Applicable Regulations	Not specified
Health Hazards	Not specified
Communications Interface Capability	Not specified
EOD Compatibility	Not specified

General

Name
ID# 36

Magnum 8000 P3, with Full Facemask

Technology	Powered respiratory system; uses internal cassette filter and can be used with P3 facemask. Magnum 8000, same as the 4000 but with audible and visual alarms for low battery or blocked filter.
Stock Number	Not specified
Protection Type	Respiratory
Equipment Category	Respirator, powered
Availability	Not specified
Current User(s)	Not specified
Manufacturer	Martindale Centurion Safety Products Ltd.
	Howlett Way
	Thetford, Norfolk
	England IP24 1HZ
	+44 (0)1842 754266 (Tel)
	+44 (0)1842 765590 (Fax)
Manufacturer Type	Foreign
Developer	Martindale Centurion Safety Products Ltd.
Source	Martindale Centurion Safety
	www.centurionsafety.co.uk
	sales@centurionsafety.co.uk
	MPS Mine and Process Service Inc.
	Box 484
	Kewanee, IL 61443
	309-852-6529 (Tel)
	309-854-5206 (Fax)
Certification	CE certified by B.S.I. to EN12941 TH3P and EN 12942 TM3P

Operational Parameters

Chemical Warfare (CW) Agents Protected Against	Not applicable
Biological Warfare (BW) Agents Protected Against	Not applicable
Toxic Industrial Materials (TIMs) Protected Against	Will protect against TIMs of toxic dust when fitted with P3 filter
Duration of Protection	Up to 2 h
Recommended Use(s)	Not specified

Physical Parameters

Sizes Available	Not specified
Weight	Not specified
Package Size and Volume	Not specified

Power Requirements	Not specified
Material Type	Not specified
Construction Type	Not specified
Color	Not specified

Logistical Parameters

Ease of Use	Easily manageable, able to be worn for long periods with no effects
Consumables	Not specified
Maintenance Requirements	Not specified
Shelf Life	Not specified
Transportability	Not specified
Operational Limitations	Not limiting, has 75 % to 90 % visibility
Environmental Conditions	Protects in normal environments
Unit Cost	Less than or equal to $500 per unit
Maintenance Cost	Not specified
Warranty	Not specified
Don/Doff Information	Not specified
Use/Reuse	Able to be cleaned and reused greater than 50 times
Launderability	Not specified
Accessories	Not specified

Special Requirements

Training Requirements	Little to no training required
Training Available	Not specified
Manuals Available	Not specified
Surveillance Testing Requirements	Not specified
Support Equipment	Not specified
Testing Information	Not specified
Applicable Regulations	Not specified
Health Hazards	Not specified
Communications Interface Capability	Not specified
EOD Compatibility	Not specified

General
Name
ID# 37

Magnum 8500 P3, with Full Facemask

Technology
Powered respiratory system. Fitted with DIN 40 thread for externally mounted screw threaded filter canister. Magnum 8500, same as the 4500 but with alarms.

Stock Number
Not specified

Protection Type
Respiratory

Equipment Category
Respirator/powered

Availability
Not specified

Current User(s)
Not specified

Manufacturer
Martindale Centurion Safety Products Ltd.
Howlett Way
Thetford, Norfolk
England IP24 1HZ
+44 (0)1842 754266 (Tel)
+44 (0)1842 765590 (Fax)

Manufacturer Type
Not specified

Developer
Martindale Centurion Safety Products Ltd.

Source
Martindale Centurion Safety
www.centurionsafety.co.uk
sales@centurionsafety.co.uk
MPS Mine and Process Service Inc.
Box 484
Kewanee, IL 61443
309-852-6529 (Tel)
309-854-5206 (Fax)

Certification
CE certified by B.S.I. to EN12941 TH3P and EN 12942 TM3P

Operational Parameters

Chemical Warfare (CW) Agents Protected Against
Not applicable

Biological Warfare (BW) Agents Protected Against
Not applicable

Toxic Industrial Materials (TIMs) Protected Against
Will protect against TIMs of toxic dust when fitted with P3 filter

Duration of Protection
Up to 2 h

Recommended Use(s)
Not specified

Physical Parameters

Sizes Available	Not specified
Weight	Not specified
Package Size and Volume	Not specified
Power Requirements	Not specified
Material Type	Not specified
Construction Type	Not specified
Color	Not specified

Logistical Parameters

Ease of Use	Easily manageable, able to be worn for long periods with no effects
Consumables	Not specified
Maintenance Requirements	Not specified
Shelf Life	Not specified
Transportability	Not specified
Operational Limitations	Not limiting, has 75 % to 90 % visibility
Environmental Conditions	Protects in normal environments
Unit Cost	Less than or equal to $500 per unit
Maintenance Cost	Not specified
Warranty	Not specified
Don/Doff Information	Not specified
Use/Reuse	Able to be cleaned and reused greater than 50 times
Launderability	Not specified
Accessories	Not specified

Special Requirements

Training Requirements	Little to no training required
Training Available	Not specified
Manuals Available	Not specified
Surveillance Testing Requirements	Not specified
Support Equipment	Not specified
Testing Information	Not specified
Applicable Regulations	Not specified
Health Hazards	Not specified
Communications Interface Capability	Not specified
EOD Compatibility	Not specified

General
Name
ID# 38

Technology

Hose system; fresh-air supply equipment. CE approved to EN138, Class 2, powered fresh-air system allows the wearer to operate in a confined area for longer periods than unpowered equipment permits, or to do heavier tasks, including work in dangerous or toxic areas which may be deficient in oxygen. Utilizing the same full facemask, waist-mounted hose coupling and 9 m hose, as the unpowered system, the Mini Turbine powered system has a twin hose for fitting on the facemask incorporating an overflow valve to allow excessive air to escape. The intake strainer at the end of the unpowered hose is removed and attached to the powered Mini Turbine and is then connected to an electrical supply. Alternative powered hoses are available from 10 m to 40 m in length. The Mini Turbine, which can be placed up to 40 m from the contaminated area, draws air from the immediate vicinity through a coarse, washable sponge filter and delivers air through a hose to one or two users.

Stock Number

TH3P/TM3P classification

Protection Type

Respiratory

Equipment Category

Hose system; fresh-air supply equipment

Availability

Not specified

Current User(s)

Not specified

Manufacturer

Martindale Centurion Safety Products Ltd.
Howlett Way
Thetford, Norfolk
England IP24 1Hz
+44 (0)1842 754266 (Tel)
+44 (0)1842 765590 (Fax)

Manufacturer Type

Foreign

Developer

Martindale Centurion Safety Products Ltd.

Source

Martindale Centurion Safety
www.centurionsafety.co.uk
sales@centurionsafety.co.uk
MPS Mine and Process Service Inc.
Box 484
Kewanee, IL 61443
309–852–6529 (Tel)
309–854–5206 (Fax)

Certification

CE certified to EN138 TH3P Class 2 by B.S.

Operational Parameters
Chemical Warfare (CW)
Agents Protected Against

Not applicable

Biological Warfare (BW) Agents Protected Against	Not applicable
Toxic Industrial Materials (TIMs) Protected Against	Will protect against TIMs of toxic dust when fitted with P3 filter; will protect against certain levels of gas
Duration of Protection	Up to 2 h
Recommended Use(s)	Not specified

Physical Parameters

Sizes Available	Not specified
Weight	Not specified
Package Size and Volume	Not specified
Power Requirements	Not specified
Material Type	Not specified
Construction Type	Not specified
Color	Not specified

Logistical Parameters

Ease of Use	Easily manageable, able to be worn for long periods with no effects
Consumables	Not specified
Maintenance Requirements	Not specified
Shelf Life	Not specified
Transportability	Not specified
Operational Limitations	Not limiting, has 75 % to 90 % visibility
Environmental Conditions	Protects in normal environments
Unit Cost	Less than or equal to $500 per unit
Maintenance Cost	Not specified
Warranty	Not specified
Don/Doff Information	Not specified
Use/Reuse	Able to be cleaned and reused greater than 50 times
Launderability	Not specified
Accessories	Not specified

Special Requirements

Training Requirements	Little to no training required
Training Available	Not specified
Manuals Available	Not specified
Surveillance Testing Requirements	Not specified
Support Equipment	Not specified
Testing Information	Not specified
Applicable Regulations	Not specified
Health Hazards	Not specified
Communications Interface Capability	Not specified
EOD Compatibility	Not specified

General

Name
ID# 39

M95 Respirator NBC Protective Respirator

Technology

Halo-butyl rubber used for the facepiece is specially engineered to enhance resistance to all known chemical and biological warfare agents. Has an exceptionally high particle filtration capacity and efficiency. Is effective against both gases and vapors, due to its high chemisorption and physisorption capacity. Has a particularly low breathing resistance NBC respiratory protection equipped with both a drinking device and a speech diaphragm. Computer-aided design for outstanding anatomical accuracy. Anatomical accuracy means that the close fit of the M95 mask offers unmatched protection. Nominal protection factor is >10000.

Stock Number
Regular: M-40007-001
Small: M40009-001

Protection Type
Respiratory

Equipment Category
Respirator, NBC protective. Practical Design and Construction: excellent fit and user comfort are the result of computer-aided design (CAD). Anatomical accuracy of the design is based on a wealth of facial form data. Facepiece has filter connections on both sides in order to facilitate left- or right-handed operation. Spectacle frames for prescription lenses. Hoseless, leakproof drinking device; intake of liquid 250 ml/min.

Availability
Commercial

Current User(s)
Finnish Armed Services

Manufacturer
Micronel Safety
5703 Industry Lane
Frederick, MD 21704
301-624-5600 (Tel)
888-744-6462 (Tel)
301-624-5688 (Fax)

Manufacturer Type
Domestic

Developer
Micronel Safety

Source
Micronel Safety Brochure
Frank Schneider, VP of Sales
fshneider@micronelsafety.com
www.lifesafetysys.com

Certification
Not specified

Operational Parameters

Chemical Warfare (CW) Agents Protected Against
Provides chemical warfare protection against agents like sarin, other nerve agents and mustard gas, cyanogen, arsine, and phosgene

Biological Warfare (BW) Agents Protected Against
Provides protection against bacteria and viruses

Toxic Industrial Materials (TIMs) Protected Against	Provides protection against many toxic industrial chemicals, gases, organic gases and vapors, inorganic gases and vapors, e.g., chlorine, hydrogen cyanide, hydrogen sulphide; organic and inorganic acids, like formic acid, sulphur dioxide, hydrogen fluoride and hydrogen chloride. Also provides protection against radioactive and highly toxic particles and aerosols.
Duration of Protection	> 48 h against CW agents
Recommended Use(s)	Provides NBC protection and meets the most critical hazards and stresses encountered in combat situations

Physical Parameters

Sizes Available	Regular and small
Weight	500 g; with filter 720 g
Package Size and Volume	Dimensions of the filter: 3.5 in height, 4.3 in diameter, and 8.8 oz
Power Requirements	Not specified.
Material Type	Halo-butyl rubber used for the facepiece is specially engineered to enhance resistance to all known chemical and biological warfare agents. Silicone inner mask provides comfortable fit against the skin. All materials are tested to withstand demanding field operations. Elastic head harness is resistant to chemicals and aging. The filter canister is made from reinforced polyamide for high impact resistance. Excellent fire retardant properties.
Construction Type	Anatomical accuracy is based on facial-form data. Facepiece has filter connections on both sides in order to facilitate left- or right-handed operation. Spectacle frames for prescription lenses. Hoseless, and leakproof drinking device.
Color	Not specified.

Logistical Parameters

Ease of Use	Excellent fit and user comfort
Consumables	Micronel Safety NBC Filter
Maintenance Requirements	Maintenance is simple to learn because the design, including the vital exhalation valve, is easy to dismantle. Replacement of the valves can be done without aid of tools.
Shelf Life	20 yr
Transportability	Not specified
Operational Limitations	Due to extremely low breathing resistance, the M95 mask and filter are comfortable to wear even for long periods, without affecting user performance. Small inner mask reduces dead-space to a minimum (CO_2 content of the M95 mask is 0.7 %). Extremely wide field of vision; even downwards; due to the close-fitting design of the mask. The stretch properties of the polyester/Lycra head-harness enhance wearer comfort, particularly over long periods.
Environmental Conditions	Temperature range is from –58 °F to +150 °F. All materials are tested to withstand demanding field operations. Excellent fire retardant properties.
Unit Cost	$325
Maintenance Cost	Not specified
Warranty	Not specified
Don/Doff Information	Donning test: 10 s
Use/Reuse	Not specified
Launderability	Not specified

ID# 39

Accessories

Spectacle frames for prescription lenses. Hoseless, leakproof drinking device, and #8211; intake of liquid 250 ml/min. Replaceable parts are color-coded to highlight vital components. Easy-to-use drinking tube for ingestion of liquids. Stability of the facepiece is ensured by chin support. NBC mask M95 for NBC respiratory protection is equipped with both a drinking device and a speech diaphragm.

Special Requirements

Training Requirements

Products must be used only by qualified persons trained in their use and maintenance and in strict accordance with and adherence to detailed instructions and precautionary statements provided in instruction manual

Training Available

Instruction manual

Manuals Available

User manual with each product

Surveillance Testing Requirements

Inspection of the valves can be carried out without the aid of tools

Support Equipment

Micronel Safety NBC filter

Testing Information

Not specified

Applicable Regulations

Not specified

Health Hazards

Not specified

Communications Interface Capability

Mask is compatible with communications devices. Speech diaphragm.

EOD Compatibility

Compatible with tactical equipment used in field operations, e.g., optical and communication devices or weapons as well as CWA protective clothing and safety helmets

General
Name
ID# 40

MSA Advantage 1000 CBA/RCA Full-Face Respirator

Technology

When the wearer inhales, contaminated air enters and flows through the cartridges, which remove the contaminants from the air stream, so the wearer breaths in clean fresh air. The Advantage 1000 Full-Face Respirator features a wrap-around flexible lens that offers a comfortable fit with increased vision. It weighs 40 % less than conventional full-face respirators and uses the same cartridges as the Advantage 200 Respirator.

Stock Number

Small: 813860
Medium: 813859
Large: 813861

Protection Type

Respiratory

Equipment Category

Respirator, full face

Availability

Commercially available

Current User(s)

Multiple cities, State governments, Federal agencies, etc.

Manufacturer

Mine Safety Appliances (MSA) Company
Defense Products Department
P.O. Box 428
Pittsburgh, PA 15230-0428

Manufacturer Type

Domestic

Developer

Mine Safety Appliances (MSA) Company

Source

Mine Safety Appliances (MSA) Company
POC: Evan K. Erickson
724-733-9274 (Tel)
724-733-8573 (Fax)
evan.erickson@msanet.com

Certification

NIOSH/MSHA-approved (no. TC-14G-0235) for protection against chloroacetophenone (CN), chlorobenzylidene (CS), P100 particulate efficiency level, and particulates

Operational Parameters
Chemical Warfare (CW) Agents Protected Against

Effective against biological agents and chemical agents GA, GD, VX, Mustard and Lewisite. Full range of CW agents; nerve, blister, and choking. Canister contains ASZM-TEDA carbon (same carbon as the C2A1 canister).

Biological Warfare (BW) Agents Protected Against

All known biological agents. Prefilter has the same level of protection as the C2A1 canister.

Toxic Industrial Materials (TIMs) Protected Against	CN, CS, P100 particulate efficiency level, and particulates. The canister has the same limitations as the C2A1, (i.e., not effective against ammonia).
Duration of Protection	Protection duration cannot be determined due to the indeterminable exposure
Recommended Use(s)	Riot control and response to terrorist incident

Physical Parameters

Sizes Available	Small, medium, and large (adult) sizes available
Weight	1.5 lb
Package Size and Volume	10 in x 6 in x 6 in
Power Requirements	No power requirements for mask alone. ESP voice projection unit is available (requires a 9 V battery to operate).
Material Type	40 % lighter than conventional full-face respirators. Mask is constructed of semi-permeable materials (a natural/nitrile blend of rubber and a polyurethane lens). Not recommended for exposure to flames or high heat. The Advantage 1000 Respirator is constructed of super-soft Hycar rubber that provides the feel and comfort of silicone but with better permeation resistance. For exceptional fit, the facepiece is available in three sizes and has a unique in-turned lip seal that provides the best possible seal against a wide range of facial contours. The Advantage 1000 facepiece also features a distinctive, flexible urethane lens that is integrally bonded to the facepiece, eliminating the need for rigid lens retainers that cause unwanted pressure points.
Construction Type	The lens is chemically bonded to the mask. Flexible, one-piece polyurethane lens with wide field of vision is bonded to durable Hycar rubber facepiece.
Color	Lens is clear, and the mask is black.

Logistical Parameters

Ease of Use	Fully elastic, six-point head harness promotes easy on-off, easy adjustment, no hair pulling. Dual-canister mount allows weapon sighting from either shoulder. Standard nosecup helps eliminate lens fogging.
Consumables	Cartridges are available with or without P100 (particulate protection): GMA P 100 Cartridge (organic vapor, P100) GME P 100 Cartridge (organic vapor, acid gases, ammonia, methylamine, formaldehyde, hydrogen fluoride, P100) GMB P 100 (acid gases, P100)
Maintenance Requirements	No service required, only periodic inspection and cleaning
Shelf Life	Mask has an indefinite shelf life if properly stored, canister has a 4 yr shelf life
Transportability	Fully transportable, can be carried on person in a belt mounted carrier
Operational Limitations	Product holds up well to type police/fire service/HAZMAT environments
Environmental Conditions	No different performance than other gas masks
Unit Cost	Masks with one canister $115 on GSA, $174 list Canisters (box of 6) $122 on GSA, $185 list
Maintenance Cost	None
Warranty	Standard commercial warranty
Don/Doff Information	No, donning can be performed by the individual
Use/Reuse	Mask can be deconned, replacement of canister is recommended
Launderability	Item is laundered, with no deterioration

Accessories

Standard equipment includes a speaking diaphragm for clear, short-range communications, and nosecup to reduce lens fogging. Additional accessories: ESP voice projection unit, clear and tinted outsert lenses, spectacle kit, butyl hood, and carrier.

Special Requirements

Training Requirements

Training requires quantitative/qualitative fit testing and initial donning instruction (<15 min) and periodic training

Training Available

None, not that complicated

Manuals Available

User manual included with each mask

Surveillance Testing Requirements

Periodic inspection required

Support Equipment

Fit test equipment, lens outsert, butyl-coated nylon hood, and carrier

Testing Information

Available from MSA appears on data sheet 05–00–03

Applicable Regulations

None

Health Hazards

None

Communications Interface Capability

ESP communications system

EOD Compatibility

Not specified

General

Name
ID# 41

MSA Advantage 1000 with GME-P100 Cartridges

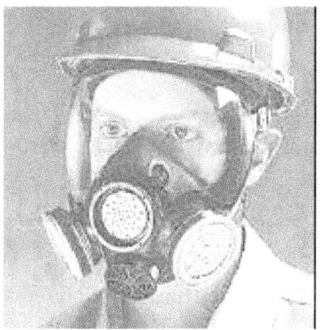

Technology

Respirator; Gas Mask
Canister contains pleated HEPA filter to remove aerosols and solid particulates and an impregnated activated carbon bed to adsorb gases and liquid vapors

Stock Number

Small: 805414
Medium: 805408
Large: 805420
815366 GME-P100 cartridges (pair)

Protection Type

Respiratory

Equipment Category

Respirator, gas mask

Availability

Commercially available

Current User(s)

Multiple cities, State governments, Federal agencies, etc.

Manufacturer

Mine Safety Appliances (MSA) Company
Defense Products Department
P.O. Box 428
Pittsburgh, PA 15230-0428

Manufacturer Type

Domestic

Developer

Mine Safety Appliances (MSA) Company

Source

Mine Safety Appliances (MSA) Company
POC: Evan K. Erickson
724-733-9274 (Tel)
724-733-8573 (Fax)
evan.erickson@msanet.com

Certification

Product is NIOSH-approved for all industrial chemicals.
Millennium used standard 40 mm thread size so have option of using NATO-style gas mask canister (however, NIOSH certification valid only with Millennium canister).

Operational Parameters

Chemical Warfare (CW) Agents Protected Against

Effective against nerve and blister agent groups. Tested using the CASHPAC protocol.

Biological Warfare (BW) Agents Protected Against

All known biological agents. Prefilter has the same level of protection as the C2A1 canister.

Toxic Industrial Materials (TIMs) Protected Against

The respirator has NIOSH approvals for all industrial chemical groups

Duration of Protection

Exceeds the 8 hr requirements of the NIOSH protocols

Recommended Use(s)

Protection against TIMs

Physical Parameters

Sizes Available	Small, medium, and large (adult) sizes available
Weight	1.8 lb
Package Size and Volume	10 in x 6 in x 6 in
Power Requirements	No power requirements for mask alone. ESP voice projection unit is available (requires a 9 V battery to operate).
Material Type	Mask is constructed of semi-permeable materials (a natural/nitrile blend of rubber and a polyurethane lens). Not recommended for exposure to flames or high heat.
Construction Type	The lens is chemically bonded to the mask
Color	Lens is clear, and the mask is black

Logistical Parameters

Ease of Use	Advantage 1000 is as functional as, if not better, than any other gas mask
Consumables	Cartridges are available with or without P100 (particulate protection): GMA P 100 Cartridge (organic vapor, P100) GME P 100 Cartridge (organic vapor, acid gases, ammonia, methylamine, formaldehyde, hydrogen fluoride, and P100) GMB P 100 (acid gases, and P100)
Maintenance Requirements	No service required, only periodic inspection and cleaning
Shelf Life	Mask has an indefinite shelf life if properly stored, cartridges have an indefinite shelf life
Transportability	Fully transportable, can be carried on person in a belt mounted carrier
Operational Limitations	Product holds up well to type police/fire service/HAZMAT environments
Environmental Conditions	No different performance than other gas masks
Unit Cost	Masks $64 on GSA, $97 list Cartridges (pair) $9.87 on GSA, $14.95 list
Maintenance Cost	None
Warranty	Standard commercial warranty
Don/Doff Information	No, donning can be performed by the individual
Use/Reuse	Mask can be deconned, replacement of cartridges is recommended
Launderability	Item is laundered, with no deterioration
Accessories	Standard equipment includes a speaking diaphragm for clear, short-range communications, and nosecup to reduce lens fogging. Additional accessories: ESP voice projection unit, clear and tinted outsert lenses, spectacle kit, and carrier.

Special Requirements

Training Requirements	Training requires quantitative/qualitative fit testing and initial donning instruction (<15 min) and periodic training
Training Available	None, not that complicated
Manuals Available	User manual included with each mask
Surveillance Testing Requirements	Periodic inspection required
Support Equipment	Fit test equipment, lens outsert, butyl-coated nylon hood, and carrier
Testing Information	Available from MSA appears on data sheet 10–00–05
Applicable Regulations	None

Health Hazards   None

Communications Interface   ESP communications system
Capability
EOD Compatibility   Not specified

General
Name
ID# 42

MSA Millennium Chemical-Biological Mask

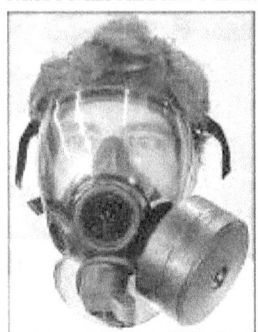

Technology
A Hycar version of the reliable military-style gas mask. Gas Mask. Canister contains pleated HEPA filter to remove aerosols and solid particulates and an impregnated activated carbon bed to adsorb gases and liquid vapors.

Stock Number
Small: 10007423
Medium: 10007422
Large: 10007424

Protection Type
Respiratory

Equipment Category
Respirator, gas mask

Availability
Commercially available

Current User(s)
Multiple cities, State governments, Federal agencies, etc. Used by Air Force in Desert Storm.

Manufacturer
Mine Safety Appliances (MSA) Company
Defense Products Department
P.O. Box 428
Pittsburgh, PA 15230-0428

Manufacturer Type
Domestic

Developer
Mine Safety Appliances (MSA) Company

Source
Mine Safety Appliances (MSA) Company
POC: Evan K. Erickson
724-733-9274 (Tel)
724-733-8573 (Fax)
evan.erickson@msanet.com

Certification
NIOSH is currently evaluating this mask for protection against chloroacetophenone (CN), chlorobenzylidene (CS), P100 particulate efficiency level, and particulates

Operational Parameters
Chemical Warfare (CW) Agents Protected Against
Full range of CW agents: GA, GD, VX, and Mustard; nerve, blister, and choking. Canister contains ASZM-TEDA carbon (same carbon as the C2A1 canister).

Biological Warfare (BW) Agents Protected Against
All known biological agents. Prefilter has the same level of protection as the C2A1 canister.

Toxic Industrial Materials (TIMs) Protected Against
CN, CS, P100 particulate efficiency level, and particulates. The canister has the same limitations as the C2A1, (i.e., not effective against ammonia).

Duration of Protection
Protection duration cannot be determined due to the indeterminable exposure

Recommended Use(s)
Riot control and response to terrorist incidents

Physical Parameters

Sizes Available	Small, medium, and large (adult) sizes available
Weight	1.6 lb
Package Size and Volume	10 in x 6 in x 6 in
Power Requirements	No power requirements for mask alone. ESP voice projection unit is available (requires a 9 V battery to operate)
Material Type	Mask is constructed of semi-permeable materials (a natural/nitrile blend of rubber and a polyurethane lens). Not recommended for exposure to flames or high heat.
Construction Type	Flexible, one-piece polyurethane lens with wide field of vision bonded to durable Hycar rubber facepiece
Color	Lens is clear, and the mask is black

Logistical Parameters

Ease of Use	Fully elastic, six-point head harness promotes easy on-off, easy adjustment, no hair pulling
Consumables	Cartridges are available with or without P100 (particulate protection): GMA P 100 Cartridge (organic vapor, and P100) GME P 100 Cartridge (organic vapor, acid gases, ammonia, methylamine, formaldehyde, hydrogen fluoride, and P100) GMB P 100 (acid gases, and P100) GMC P 100 (organic vapor, acid gases, and P100) GMD P 100 (ammonia, methylamine, and P100) Mersorb Cartridge P 100 Cartridge (chlorine, mercury vapor, and P100) R95 Prefilter and Cover (add to cartridge to achieve R95 rating)
Maintenance Requirements	No service required, only periodic inspection and cleaning
Shelf Life	Mask has an indefinite shelf life if properly stored, canister has a 4 yr shelf life
Transportability	Fully transportable, can be carried on person in a belt mounted carrier
Operational Limitations	Product holds up well to type police/fire service/HAZMAT environments
Environmental Conditions	No different performance than other gas masks
Unit Cost	Masks with one canister $184 on GSA, $297 list Canisters (box of 6) $102 on GSA, $210 list
Maintenance Cost	None
Warranty	Standard commercial warranty
Don/Doff Information	No, donning can be performed by the individual
Use/Reuse	Mask can be deconned, replacement of canister is recommended
Launderability	Item is laundered, with no deterioration
Accessories	Standard equipment includes a speaking diaphragm for clear, short-range communications, and nosecup to reduce lens fogging. Additional accessories: ESP voice projection unit, clear and tinted outsert lenses, spectacle kit, butyl hood, and carrier. Drinking tube.

Special Requirements

Training Requirements	Training requires quantitative/qualitative fit testing and initial donning instruction (<15 min) and periodic training.
Training Available	None, not that complicated.
Manuals Available	User manual included with each mask
Surveillance Testing Requirements	Periodic inspection required

Support Equipment	Fit test equipment, lens outsert, butyl-coated nylon hood, and carrier. Internal nosecup with 2 check valves deflects air from the lens, reduces fogging. Standard mechanical speaking diaphragm included.
Testing Information	Available from MSA appears on data sheet 05–00–03
Applicable Regulations	None
Health Hazards	None
Communications Interface Capability	ESP communications system
EOD Compatibility	Not specified

General

Name
ID# 43

MSA OptimAir® MM 2K PAPR

Technology

The unit filters particulates and provides respirable air directly to the Ultravue or Ultra Elite Facepiece. Since it does not have a breathing tube, the unit is more compact than other PAPRs, enhancing user maneuverability and simplifying decontamination. OptimAir* MM 2K PAPR with Type HE OptiFilter* XL Cartridge is smaller, lighter, and less expensive, thanks largely to a new NiMH battery pack and dual-rate smart charger. The low-profile NiMH (nickel metal hydride) battery pack is lightweight (12.5 oz.), fits close to the body, and is small enough to fit in most pockets. The battery provides 8 h of continuous use, lasting a full work shift. Another benefit is that NiMH batteries do not have a "memory effect" like NiCad batteries. The sealed, water-resistant battery pack is designed for easy shower decontamination. The dual-rate smart charger is a standard accessory with this unit. The charger can recharge a battery in less than 3 h. An LED indicates battery condition: fast charge, fully charged, or battery fault. The lightweight, compact design of the OptimAir MM 2K PAPR is well suited for abatement, nuclear, and other industries with hazardous particulate environments. The water-resistant filter has an optional prefilter and cover. Complete units include motor/blower, NiMH battery, dual-rate charger, one Type HE OptiFilter XL Cartridge, urethane-coated nylon web belt, and choice of Ultravue or Ultra Elite Facepiece. The "2K PAPR" is a direct replacement for the OptimAir MM PAPR.

Stock Number
10023569

Protection Type
Respiratory

Equipment Category
PAPR/cartridge

Availability
Commercially available

Current User(s)
Asbestos abatement, chemical, electric utility, nuclear, paper and pulp, sanding and grinding, and welding

Manufacturer
Mine Safety Appliances (MSA) Company
Defense Products Department
P.O. Box 428
Pittsburgh, PA 15230-0428

Manufacturer Type
Domestic

Developer
Mine Safety Appliances (MSA) Company

Source
Mine Safety Appliances (MSA) Company
POC: Evan K. Erickson
724-733-9274 (Tel)
724-733-8573 (Fax)
evan.erickson@msanet.com

Certification
Approvals and standards
Various NIOSH approval numbers based on facepiece or hood style

Operational Parameters

Chemical Warfare (CW) Agents Protected Against
GMA-H cartridge

Biological Warfare (BW) Agents Protected Against
P100 particulate filter

Toxic Industrial Materials (TIMs) Protected Against
Particulate and dust, toxic atmosphere non-IDLH, and welding

Duration of Protection
8 h

Recommended Use(s)
Designed to filter contaminants from ambient air and provide constant air flow to facepiece

Physical Parameters

Sizes Available
Three sizes

Weight
< 4 lb

Package Size and Volume
1 ft³

Power Requirements
NiMH battery, dual-rate charger; low-profile NiMH (nickel metal hydride) battery pack is lightweight (12.5 oz)

Material Type
Ultravue facepiece, medium, black, and Hycar rubber

Construction Type
Rubber facepiece with polycarbonate lens, mask mounted blower and cartridge, and belt mounted battery pack

Color
Lens is clear

Logistical Parameters

Ease of Use
Easy adjustment

Consumables
Combination of cartridges for protection against particulates, toxic gases and vapors, or a combination of these hazards

Maintenance Requirements
Maintenance-free lithium battery

Shelf Life
5 yr

Transportability
Fully transportable

Operational Limitations
Product holds up well in police/HAZMAT type environments

Environmental Conditions
Typical respirator

Unit Cost
$326 GSA, $494 list

Maintenance Cost
None

Warranty
Standard commercial warranty

Don/Doff Information
No, donning can be performed by the individual

Use/Reuse
Can be deconned, canister replacement recommended

Launderability
Easy shower decontamination

Accessories
Complete units include motor/blower, NiMH battery, dual-rate charger, one type HE OptiFilter XL cartridge, urethane-coated nylon web belt, and choice of Ultravue or Ultra Elite facepiece

Special Requirements

Training Requirements
Minimal

Training Available
Video tape

Manuals Available
Manuals included with product

Surveillance Testing Requirements
Periodic inspection

Support Equipment
Protective covers

Testing Information
Data sheet available from MSA

Applicable Regulations	NIOSH-approved
Health Hazards	None
Communications Interface Capability	None
EOD Compatibility	Not specified

General

Name
ID# 44

MSA OptimAir* 6A PAPR with OptiFilter Cartridges

Technology

The OptimAir 6A PAPR provides respiratory protection by filtering contaminants from ambient air and providing a constant air flow to either a facepiece or hood (with CBA/RCA or HEPA filters) at a rate equal to or exceeding NIOSH standards. Can be used with an entire family of filters, chemical cartridges and combination cartridges for protection against particulates, toxic gases and vapors or a combination of these hazards. It requires two filters. The unit is available with full- or half-mask facepieces, or hood. The belt-mounted motor/blower assembly includes a highly efficient 4.6 V motor that has a long service life. The motor/blower assembly features threaded connectors for quick and easy attachment of OptiFilter Cartridges.

Stock Number

00749: OptimAir 6A PAPR with medium, black hycar comfo half-mask facepiece
800767: OptimAir 6A PAPR with medium, black hycar comfo welder's half-mask
1001890: CBA/RCA canisters

Protection Type
Respiratory

Equipment Category
PAPR, with HEPA filters

Availability
Commercially available

Current User(s)
Asbestos abatement, chemical, electric utility, hazardous materials, nuclear, oil and gas, paper and pulp, and sanding and grinding

Manufacturer
Mine Safety Appliances (MSA) Company
Defense Products Department
P.O. Box 428
Pittsburgh, PA 15230-0428

Manufacturer Type
Domestic

Developer
Mine Safety Appliances (MSA) Company

Source
Mine Safety Appliances (MSA) Company
POC: Evan K. Erickson
724-733-9274 (Tel)
724-733-8573 (Fax)
evan.erickson@msanet.com

Certification
The OptimAir 6A Powered Air-Purifying Respirator with Ultravue, Comfo Elite, or Comfo Welder's Facepieces or Tyvek Hood has approvals from the National Institute for Occupational Safety and Health (NIOSH) and Mine Safety and Health Administration (MSHA). Filters and cartridges are covered by separate approval. Cartridges must be replaced whenever air flow drops below 4 cubic ft per min (115 lpm) with tight-fitting facepieces or 6 cubic ft per min (170 lpm) with the Tyvek hood, or when the user smells or tastes the contaminant.

Operational Parameters

Chemical Warfare (CW) Agents Protected Against

Effective against biological agents and chemical agents: GA, GD, VX, Mustard, and Lewisite. Full range of CW agents; nerve, blister, and choking. Canister contains ASZM-TEDA carbon (same carbon as the C2A1 canister).

Biological Warfare (BW) Agents Protected Against

All known biological agents. Prefilter has the same level of protection as the C2A1 canister.

Toxic Industrial Materials (TIMs) Protected Against

Particulate and dust, toxic atmosphere non-IDLH, and welding

Duration of Protection

Protection duration cannot be determined due to the indeterminable exposure

Recommended Use(s)

Designed to filter contaminants from ambient air and provide constant air flow to facepiece

Physical Parameters

Sizes Available — Full-face Hycar rubber Ultravue Facepeice in three sizes

Weight — 8 lb

Package Size and Volume — 1.5 ft^3

Power Requirements — 1500 h brush-type motor in a motor/blower module; lithium battery; operational battery, and charger

Material Type — Ultravue facepiece, medium, black, and Hycar rubber

Construction Type — Rubber mask with lens, rubber breathing tube, and belt mounted blower/cartridges

Color — Lens is clear

Logistical Parameters

Ease of Use — Fully elastic, six-point head harness promotes easy on-off, easy adjustment, no hair pulling. Dual-canister mount allows weapon sighting from either shoulder. Standard nosecup helps eliminate lens fogging.

Consumables — Combination of cartridges for protection against particulates, toxic gases and vapors, or a combination of these hazards

Maintenance Requirements — Maintenance-free lithium battery

Shelf Life — Maintenance free lithium battery with 10 yr shelf life

Transportability — Fully transportable

Operational Limitations — Product holds up well to type police/fire service/HAZMAT environments

Environmental Conditions — No different performance than other gas masks

Unit Cost — OptimAir 6A PAPR—$445 GSA, $674 list

Maintenance Cost — None

Warranty — Standard commercial warranty

Don/Doff Information — No, donning can be performed by the individual

Use/Reuse — Mask can be deconned, and replacement of canister is recommended

Launderability — Item is laundered, with no deterioration

Accessories — Tyvek hood shell, less Simple Hood Suspension 488721
Battery pack 491120
OptimAir 6A PAPR with Tyvek hood, two Type H OptiFilter XL Cartridges, motor/blower, battery, belt, and battery charger 49130, Polyurethane-coated Nylon-Web Belt 492827
Air-purifying Respirator with Ultravue Facepiece, lithium battery, belt, and motor/blower module

Special Requirements

Training Requirements	Training requires quantitative/qualitative fit testing and initial donning instruction (<15 min) and periodic training
Training Available	None, not that complicated
Manuals Available	User manual included with each mask
Surveillance Testing Requirements	Periodic inspection
Support Equipment	Protective covers, facepiece, motor/blower, battery, belt, and battery charger
Testing Information	Data sheet available from MSA
Applicable Regulations	None
Health Hazards	None
Communications Interface Capability	None
EOD Compatibility	Not specified

General
Name
ID# 45

MSA Phalanx CBA/RCA Gas Mask

Technology

Canister contains pleated HEPA filter to remove aerosols and solid particulates and an impregnated activated carbon bed to adsorb gases and liquid vapors. The Phalanx facepiece has canister inlet ports on both sides of facepiece.

Stock Number

Small: 487330
Medium: 487329
Large: 487331

Protection Type

Respiratory

Equipment Category

Gas Mask

Availability

Product is in production

Current User(s)

Multiple cities, State governments, Federal agencies, etc.

Manufacturer

Mine Safety Appliances (MSA) Company
Defense Products Department
P.O. Box 428
Pittsburgh, PA 15230-0428

Manufacturer Type

Domestic

Developer

Mine Safety Appliances (MSA) Company

Source

Mine Safety Appliances (MSA) Company
POC: Evan K. Erickson
724-733-9274 (Tel)
724-733-8573 (Fax)
evan.erickson@msanet.com

Certification

Product is NIOSH-approved (No. TC-14G-0236) for chlorobenzylidene (CS) and chloracetophenone (CN) tear gasses, P100 particulate efficiency level, and particulates

Operational Parameters
Chemical Warfare (CW) Agents Protected Against

Full range of CW agents; GA, CB (Sarin), GD, VX, Mustard, and Lewisite. Canister contains ASZM-TEDA carbon (same carbon as the C2A1 canister).

Biological Warfare (BW) Agents Protected Against

All known BW agents. Prefilter has the same level of protection as the C2A1 canister.

Toxic Industrial Materials (TIMs) Protected Against

Toxic Atmosphere non-IDLH
The canister has the same limitations as the C2A1, (i.e., not effective against ammonia)

Duration of Protection

Protection duration cannot be determined due to the indeterminable exposure

Recommended Use(s)

Protection against riot control agents. Phalanx CBA-RCA (Chemical/Biological Agent-Riot Control Agent) Gas Masks from MSA are specifically designed for use by law enforcement and emergency response personnel.

Physical Parameters

Sizes Available
Small, medium, and large (adult) sizes available

Weight
1.6 lb

Package Size and Volume
10 in x 6 in x 6 in

Power Requirements
No power requirements for mask alone. ESP voice projection unit is available (requires a 9 V battery to operate).

Material Type
Gas Masks are molded from black Hycar rubber, a specially formulated combination of natural rubber and synthetic materials. The facepiece is soft and pliable for a snug, comfortable fit. Hycar resists chemical attack and temperature extremes and is able to withstand rugged daily use. Hycar is particularly resistant to permeation against chemical warfare agents. The lens is made of polycarbonate and is coated on both sides to resist scratching and chemical attack. The facepiece has a wraparound design to minimize dead-air space and to provide good vision.

Construction Type
The lens is mechanically fastened to the mask

Color
Lens is clear, and the mask is black

Logistical Parameters

Ease of Use
EZ-Don Facepiece Harness provides quick, simple facepiece donning. A quick tug on the bottom two straps secures a snug fit. The Phalanx has been used by police forces across the nation for more than 20 yr. Minimal incompatibilities have been reported.

Consumables
Cartridges are available with or without P100 (particulate protection):
GMA P 100 Cartridge (Organic vapor, and P100)
GME P 100 Cartridge (Organic vapor, acid gases, ammonia, methylamine, formaldehyde, hydrogen fluoride, and P100)
GMB P 100 (acid gases, and P100)
GMC P 100 (organic vapor, acid gases, and P100)
GMD P 100 (ammonia, methylamine, and P100)
Mersorb cartridge P 100 cartridge (chlorine, mercury vapor, P100)
R95 prefilter and cover (add to cartridge to achieve R95 rating)

Maintenance Requirements
No service required, only periodic inspection and cleaning. Can be easily disassembled for cleaning and parts replacement.

Shelf Life
Mask has an indefinite shelf life if properly stored, canister has a 4 yr shelf life

Transportability
Fully transportable, can be carried on person in a belt mounted carrier

Operational Limitations
Product holds up well to type police/fire service/HAZMAT environments

Environmental Conditions
No different performance than other gas masks. No considerations.

Unit Cost
Masks with one canister $134 on GSA, $203 list
Canisters (box of 6) $136 on GSA, $220 list

Maintenance Cost
None

Warranty
Standard commercial warranty

Don/Doff Information
No, donning can be performed by the individual

Use/Reuse
Mask can be deconned, replacement of canister is recommended

Launderability
Item is laundered, with no deterioration

Accessories
Additional accessories: Replacement nosecups, cover lenses, MSA cleaner, replacement ID tag with cable tie, butyl-coated nylon hood, and carrier. ESP voice projection unit, clear and tinted outsert lenses, spectacle kit, butyl hood, and carrier.

Special Requirements

Training Requirements
Training requires quantitative/qualitative fit testing and initial donning instruction (<15 min) and periodic training

Training Available
None, not that complicated

Manuals Available	User manual included with each mask
Surveillance Testing Requirements	Periodic inspection
Support Equipment	Fit test equipment
Testing Information	Available from MSA appears on data sheet 05–01–03
Applicable Regulations	None
Health Hazards	None
Communications Interface Capability	The facepiece adapts to optional ESP communications system
EOD Compatibility	Not specified

General
Name
ID# 46

MSA PremAire™ XV Supplied Air Respirator

Technology

The respirator is a combination respirator that can be used as a versatile airline respirator with emergency escape capability or as a stand-alone SCBA. The respirator features a high-performance mask-mounted regulator and a pair of compact, waist-mounted air cylinders. Vortex tube body cooling and warming capability. U.S. Patent No. 5,017,807.

Stock Number
496780

Protection Type
Respiratory

Equipment Category
Combination respirator that can be stand-alone (SCBA) or airline with emergency escape capability
813729: PremAire XV Cadet Respirator complete with medium SoftFeel Rubber Ultra Elite Facepiece
813760: PremAire XV System Respirator complete with PremAire System Manifold and Medium SoftFeel Rubber Ultra Elite Facepiece

Availability
Commercially available

Current User(s)
Not specified

Manufacturer
Mine Safety Appliances (MSA) Company
Defense Products Department
P.O. Box 428
Pittsburgh, PA 15230–0428

Manufacturer Type
Domestic

Developer
Mine Safety Appliances (MSA) Company

Source
Mine Safety Appliances (MSA) Company
POC: Evan K. Erickson
724–733–9274 (Tel)
724–733–8573 (Fax)
evan.erickson@msanet.com

Certification
Approvals and Standards
NIOSH/MSHA-approved. The self-contained air-supply is approved for entry into and escape from IDLH atmospheres.

Operational Parameters
Chemical Warfare (CW) Agents Protected Against
Supplied air respirator

Biological Warfare (BW) Agents Protected Against
Supplied air respirator

Toxic Industrial Materials (TIMs) Protected Against
Toxic atmosphere IDLH

Duration of Protection	Combines the best features of an advanced, air-supplied respirator with those of a 15 min SCBA. Vortex tube body cooling and warming capability. U.S. Patent No. 5,017,807.
Recommended Use(s)	Agriculture, chemical, electric utility, hazardous materials, and paper and pulp industries

Physical Parameters

Sizes Available	Small, medium, and large facepiece
Weight	< 10 lb
Package Size and Volume	15 in x 12 in x 6 in
Power Requirements	None
Material Type	Not specified
Construction Type	Rubber mask with belt mounted cylinder/airline
Color	Black facepiece

Logistical Parameters

Ease of Use	Requires fit testing (15 min) and initial donning instruction
Consumables	Air cylinder must be refilled
Maintenance Requirements	Unopened, 6 mo
Shelf Life	5 yr
Transportability	Easily transported
Operational Limitations	Product holds up well to police/fire/HAZMAT environments
Environmental Conditions	None
Unit Cost	$389 GSA; $589 list
Maintenance Cost	None
Warranty	Standard commercial warranty
Don/Doff Information	No, donning can be performed by the individual
Use/Reuse	Can be decontaminated
Launderability	Can be laundered
Accessories	Composite cylinders and coated-nylon carrier assembly

Special Requirements

Training Requirements	15 min for fit testing and initial donning instruction
Training Available	Video
Manuals Available	Included with product
Surveillance Testing Requirements	Periodic inspection required
Support Equipment	Fit test equipment
Testing Information	Appears in MSA bulletin
Applicable Regulations	None
Health Hazards	None
Communications Interface Capability	ESP communications system
EOD Compatibility	Not specified

General
Name
ID# 47

MSA RescueAire™ II Portable Air-Supply System

Technology

The RescueAire II Portable Air-Supply System is designed to meet the needs of Rapid Intervention Teams (RITs). The system consists of a lightweight Stealth™ carbon cylinder, a Quick-Fill® emergency breathing system (EBS), an ExtendAire™ emergency breathing system, and an MMR regulator, supported by a heat- and flame-resistant carrying harness (made from Nomex and Kevlar materials). The RescueAire System allows firefighters to provide emergency breathing air for almost any victim quickly and easily. The Quick-Fill EBS allows users to refill and transfill air cylinders while the SCBA is worn, even in IDLH atmospheres. The ExtendAire System can be used both as an EBS and as a dual-purpose device for MMR SCBA to allow firefighters to connect to an air line. Built for the extreme conditions required by the Fire Service, the RescueAire II System is available in both low-pressure (2216 psig) and high-pressure (4500 psig) versions. An optional-use shoulder strap provides for hands-free carrying.

Stock Number

813729
813760

Protection Type

Respiratory

Equipment Category

SCBA, can be used as a dual-purpose device for MMR SCBA or to connect to an airline
813729: PremAire XV Cadet Respirator complete with medium SoftFeel Rubber Ultra Elite Facepiece
813760: PremAire XV System Respirator complete with PremAire System Manifold and Medium SoftFeel Rubber Ultra Elite Facepiece

Availability

Commercially available

Current User(s)

Fire Fighters

Manufacturer

Mine Safety Appliances (MSA) Company
Defense Products Department
P.O. Box 428
Pittsburgh, PA 15230–0428

Manufacturer Type

Domestic

Developer

Mine Safety Appliances (MSA) Company

Source

Mine Safety Appliances (MSA) Company
POC: Evan K. Erickson
724–733–9274 (Tel)
724–733–8573 (Fax)
evan.erickson@msanet.com

Certification

Approvals and Standards
NIOSH/MSHA-approved. The self-contained air-supply is approved for entry into and escape from IDLH atmospheres.

Operational Parameters

Chemical Warfare (CW) Agents Protected Against	Supplied air respirator
Biological Warfare (BW) Agents Protected Against	Supplied air respirator
Toxic Industrial Materials (TIMs) Protected Against	Combustible atmosphere, confined space, fire, oxygen deficiency, and toxic atmosphere IDLH
Duration of Protection	60 min
Recommended Use(s)	Built for the extreme conditions required by the Fire Service, the RescueAire II System is available in both low-pressure (2216 psig) and high-pressure (4500 psig) versions. An optional-use shoulder strap provides for hands-free carrying.

Physical Parameters

Sizes Available	60 min cylinder
Weight	12 lb
Package Size and Volume	10 in x 10 in x 24 in
Power Requirements	None
Material Type	Carbon fiber composite
Construction Type	Carbon fiber composite
Color	Natural

Logistical Parameters

Ease of Use	SCBA training required
Consumables	Cylinder must be refilled
Maintenance Requirements	None
Shelf Life	15 yr
Transportability	Easily transported
Operational Limitations	Product holds up well in all environments
Environmental Conditions	None
Unit Cost	Not specified
Maintenance Cost	None
Warranty	Standard commercial warranty
Don/Doff Information	None
Use/Reuse	Refillable
Launderability	Can be decontaminated
Accessories	Composite cylinders and coated-nylon carrier assembly

Special Requirements

Training Requirements	SCBA training required
Training Available	Video
Manuals Available	Included with product
Surveillance Testing Requirements	Periodic inspection required
Support Equipment	None
Testing Information	Data sheet available from MSA

Applicable Regulations   None
Health Hazards   None
Communications Interface   None
Capability
EOD Compatibility   Not specified

General

Name
ID# 48

MSA Ultra-Twin® Respirators

Technology

The Ultra-Twin Full-Facepiece Respirator has an in-turned lip around the edge for a tight seal against the face. A large chin cup makes it easy to position. Five suspension headstraps and roller buckles hold the facepiece in place while minimizing hair entanglement. Wide polycarbonate lens is coated to resist scratching and chemical attack. Lens is held in place by a two-piece lens ring, which is color-coded to indicate the size of the facepiece. Uses the full line of Comfo Cartridges and filters.

Stock Number
471298

Protection Type
Respiratory

Equipment Category
Respirator

Availability
Commercially available

Current User(s)
Not specified

Manufacturer
Mine Safety Appliances (MSA) Company
Defense Products Department
P.O. Box 428
Pittsburgh, PA 15230-0428

Manufacturer Type
Domestic

Developer
Mine Safety Appliances (MSA) Company

Source
Mine Safety Appliances (MSA) Company
POC: Evan K. Erickson
724-733-9274 (Tel)
724-733-8573 (Fax)
evan.erickson@msanet.com

Certification
NIOSH-approved for industrial chemicals

Operational Parameters

Chemical Warfare (CW) Agents Protected Against
Effective against nerve and blister agent groups. Tested using the CASHPAC protocol.

Biological Warfare (BW) Agents Protected Against
All known biological agents. Prefilter has the same level of protection as the C2A1 canister.

Toxic Industrial Materials (TIMs) Protected Against
Ammonia, formaldehyde, hydrogen fluoride, formaldehyde, and chlorine

Duration of Protection
Exceeds the 8 h requirements of the NIOSH protocols

Recommended Use(s)
Protection against TIMs

Physical Parameters

Sizes Available	Small, medium, and large sizes
Weight	2 lb
Package Size and Volume	10 in x 6 in x 6 in
Power Requirements	None
Material Type	Mask is rubber, lens polycarbonate
Construction Type	Mechanical assembly
Color	Black with clear lens

Logistical Parameters

Ease of Use	Comfort, and freedom of movement
Consumables	Cartridges are available with or without P100 (particulate protection): GMA P 100 Cartridge (organic vapor, and P100) GME P 100 Cartridge (organic vapor, acid gases, ammonia, methylamine, formaldehyde, hydrogen fluoride, and P100) GMB P 100 (acid gases, and P100) GMC P 100 (organic vapor, acid gases, and P100) GMD P 100 (ammonia, methylamine, and P100) Mersorb Cartridge P 100 Cartridge (chlorine, mercury vapor, and P100) R95 prefilter and cover (add to cartridge to achieve R95 rating)
Maintenance Requirements	No service required, only periodic inspection and cleaning
Shelf Life	Mask has an indefinite shelf life if properly stored, cartridges have an indefinite shelf life
Transportability	Fully transportable, can be carried on person in a belt mounted carrier
Operational Limitations	Product holds up well to type police/fire service/HAZMAT environments
Environmental Conditions	No different performance than other gas masks
Unit Cost	Masks $125 on GSA, $189 list
Maintenance Cost	None
Warranty	Standard commercial warranty
Don/Doff Information	No, donning can be performed by the individual
Use/Reuse	Mask can be deconned, replacement of cartridges is recommended
Launderability	Item can be laundered, with no deterioration
Accessories	Standard equipment includes a speaking diaphragm for clear, short-range communications, and nosecup to reduce lens fogging. Additional accessories: ESP voice projection unit, clear and tinted outsert lenses, spectacle kit, and carrier.

Special Requirements

Training Requirements	Training requires quantitative/qualitative fit testing and initial donning instruction (<15 min) and periodic training
Training Available	None, not that complicated
Manuals Available	User manual included with each mask
Surveillance Testing Requirements	Periodic inspection required
Support Equipment	Fit test equipment, lens outsert, butyl-coated nylon hood, and carrier
Testing Information	Appears in MSA bulletin
Applicable Regulations	None
Health Hazards	None

Communications Interface Capability   ESP communications system

EOD Compatibility   Not specified

General

Name
ID# 49

MSA MCU-2/P and MCU-2A/P Series

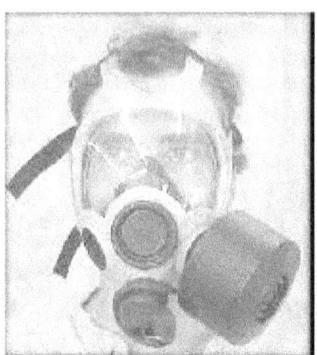

Technology Respirator/Mask; EOD protection when worn with HGU-65/P hood

Stock Number MSA:
Small - 306762
Medium - 306763
Large - 306764
Government:
Small - 4240-01-327-3299
Medium - 4240-01-327-3300
Large - 4240-01-327-3301

Protection Type Respiratory

Equipment Category Respirator, mask, and EOD protection

Availability Military

Current User(s) U.S. Air Force general purpose respirator. Also by FBI, Secret Service, Drug Enforcement Agency, Coast Guard, Department of Energy, and Navy

Manufacturer Mine Safety Appliances (MSA) Company
Defense Products Department
P.O. Box 428
Pittsburgh, PA 15230-0428

Manufacturer Type Domestic

Developer Mine Safety Appliances (MSA) Company

Source Worldwide NBC Mask Handbook
POC: Evan K. Erickson
724-733-9274 (Tel)
724-733-8573 (Fax)
evan.erickson@msanet.com

Certification Canister mount

Operational Parameters

Chemical Warfare (CW) Agents Protected Against Exceeds the required protection factor of 10(4). Protects the wearer from chemical and biological agents and radioactive dust.

Biological Warfare (BW) Agents Protected Against Exceeds the required protection factor of 10(4). Protects the wearer from chemical and biological agents and radioactive dust.

Toxic Industrial Materials (TIMs) Protected Against Limitations of C2A1

Duration of Protection Cannot predict, level of toxins determine duration

Recommended Use(s) Riot control, chemical agent, and biological agent

Physical Parameters

Sizes Available	Small, medium, and large
Weight	27 oz (facepiece and canister) 10 oz (canister) 18 oz (mask)
Package Size and Volume	10 in x 6 in x 6 in
Power Requirements	None
Material Type	Molded silicone rubber facepiece material with polyurethane one-piece panoramic lens bonded to it
Construction Type	Component(s): Drinking device, eyepiece(s) made of clear molded urethane and bonded to facepiece; facepiece (molded silicone rubber); head harness (six-point suspension); and nosecup
Color	Grey

Logistical Parameters

Ease of Use	Field of vision: Excellent optical properties including an enhanced peripheral field
Consumables	C2 canister or any other NATO standard thread canister
Maintenance Requirements	None
Shelf Life	Indefinite shelf life
Transportability	Fully transportable, can be carried on person in a belt mounted carrier
Operational Limitations	Product holds up well to type police/fire service/HAZMAT environments
Environmental Conditions	No different performance than other gas masks
Unit Cost	Mask $195; kit $300
Maintenance Cost	None
Warranty	Not specified
Don/Doff Information	Less than 9 s, an additional 6 s to don/adjust the hood
Use/Reuse	Mask can be deconned, replacement of canister is recommended
Launderability	Item can be laundered, with no deterioration
Accessories	Includes three C2 canisters: carrier (mildew-resistant nylon bag with pockets); hood(s) made of butyl rubber-coated nylon cloth; outserts (one optically clear and one tinted, both made of polycarbonate shell that can protect the wearer from chemical droplets and POLs); waterproof bag (to protect mask from moisture in wet and damp climates)

Special Requirements

Training Requirements	Required
Training Available	Not specified
Manuals Available	Not specified
Surveillance Testing Requirements	Periodic inspection required
Support Equipment	Fit test equipment; lens outsert; butyl-coated nylon hood; carrier
Testing Information	Available from MSA and appears on data sheet 05–00–03
Applicable Regulations	None
Health Hazards	None

Communications Interface Capability   ESP communications system

EOD Compatibility   EOD protection when worn with HGU-65/P hood

General

Name
ID# 50

Technology

MMR Xtreme Air Masks are pressure-demand apparatus, designed to maintain a slight positive air pressure inside the facepiece during inhalation and exhalation. This helps prevent contaminants from seeping in around the facepiece, even if there are small breaks in the face-to-facepiece seal. Sleek, rugged and lightweight, the MMR Xtreme Air Mask is the future of self-contained breathing apparatus (SCBA). Comfortable, wide-vision Ultra Elite facepiece and clean, low profile mask-mounted regulator with large shutoff button. High-strength yet lightweight cylinder options and advanced Black Rhino or Vulcan carrier/harness assembly. MMR Xtreme Air Masks are the superior options available on the Ultralite and Custom 4500 MMR Air Masks.

Stock Number

Several models available. All have medium black hycal ultra elite facepiece, 30 min rated stealth cylinder, vulcan carrier with lumbar pad and chest strap, and without case.

10018584: Ultralite MMR Xtreme Air Mask, and DragonFly IP with heat sensor

10018585: Ultralite MMR Xtreme Air Mask, quick-fill system, and DragonFly IP with heat sensor

10018586: Custom 4500 MMR Xtreme Air Mask, and DragonFly IP with heat sensor

10018587: Custom 4500 MMR Xtreme Air Mask, quick-fill system, and DragonFly IP with heat sensor

10024214: Ultralite MMR Xtreme Air Mask, and ICM 2000 with heat sensor

10024215: Ultralite MMR Xtreme Air Mask, and ICM 2000 Plus with heat sensor

10024216: Custom 4500 MMR Xtreme Air Mask, and ICM 2000 with heat sensor

10024217: Custom 4500 MMR Xtreme Air Mask, and ICM 2000 Plus with heat sensor

10024218: Custom 4500 MMR Xtreme Air Mask, quick-fill system, and ICM 2000 Plus with heat sensor

Protection Type
Respiratory

Equipment Category
SCBA, pressure-demand to maintain slight positive air pressure

Availability
Commercially available

Current User(s)
Fire fighters across the country

Manufacturer
Mine Safety Appliances (MSA) Company
Defense Products Department
P.O. Box 428
Pittsburgh, PA 15230–0428

Manufacturer Type	Domestic
Developer	Mine Safety Appliances (MSA) Company
Source	Internet
	POC: Evan K. Erickson
	724–733–9274 (Tel)
	724–733–8573 (Fax)
	evan.erickson@msanet.com
Certification	The MMR Xtreme Air Masks comply with the performance requirements of the American National Standards Institute (ANSI) and the National Fire Protection Association (NFPA) ANSI/NFPA–1981 Standard for Open-circuit SCBA, 1997 Edition. They are certified by the National Institute for Occupational Safety and Health (NIOSH).

Operational Parameters

Chemical Warfare (CW) Agents Protected Against	Supplied air respirator
Biological Warfare (BW) Agents Protected Against	Supplied air respirator
Toxic Industrial Materials (TIMs) Protected Against	Confined space, fire, oxygen deficiency, toxic atmosphere IDLH, chemical, electric utility, fire fighting, nuclear, oil, and gas
Duration of Protection	Dependent of cylinder refill capability
Recommended Use(s)	All environments

Physical Parameters

Sizes Available	Small, medium, and large facepieces; 30 min, 45 min, and 60 min air cylinders
Weight	20 lb to 30 lb
Package Size and Volume	< 2 ft^3
Power Requirements	None
Material Type	Rubber mask
Construction Type	Typical
Color	Black mask

Logistical Parameters

Ease of Use	Typical SCBA
Consumables	Cylinder must be refilled
Maintenance Requirements	Periodic service and calibration
Shelf Life	5 yr to 15 yr
Transportability	Fully transportable
Operational Limitations	Designed for police/firefighters/HAZMAT environments
Environmental Conditions	Full range of environments
Unit Cost	P/N 10018584 $2.5K GSA, $4.1K list
	Prices vary depending on options selected
Maintenance Cost	Dependent on use
Warranty	Standard commercial warranty
Don/Doff Information	No, donning can be performed by the individual
Use/Reuse	Can be decontaminated
Launderability	Item can be laundered with no deterioration
Accessories	Refer to MSA data sheet

Special Requirements

Training Requirements	Initial training, and fit testing required
Training Available	Video
Manuals Available	Included with product
Surveillance Testing Requirements	Periodic inspection required
Support Equipment	None
Testing Information	Refer to MSA data sheet
Applicable Regulations	None
Health Hazards	None
Communications Interface Capability	ESP R1 system
EOD Compatibility	Fits under EOD hoods/suits

General

Name
ID# 51

3M™ Breathe Easy™ 7 RRPAS™ Respirator

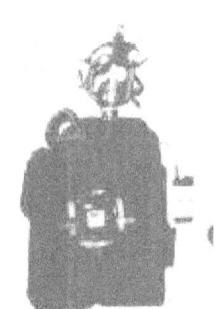

Technology | Respirator/Powered Air
Stock Number | 4240-01-447-2829
Protection Type | Respiratory
Equipment Category | Respirator, powered air
Availability | Commercially available
Current User(s) | Not specified
Manufacturer | 3M
3M Center
Bldg. 235-2W-70
St. Paul, MN 55144-1000
Manufacturer Type | Domestic
Developer | 3M
Source | 3M
POC: Jean Koecher
651-736-8272 (Tel)

Certification | NIOSH-approved for certain organic vapors, acid gases and as a high efficiency filter when used with the AEP3 cartridge (4240-01-323-3530). Approval numbers available upon request

Operational Parameters

Chemical Warfare (CW) Agents Protected Against | Contact 3M Technical Service for this information. In U.S. call 800-243-4630, in Canada call 800-267-4414

Biological Warfare (BW) Agents Protected Against | Contact 3M Technical Service for this information. In U.S. call 800-243-4630, in Canada call 800-267-4414

Toxic Industrial Materials (TIMs) Protected Against | Contact 3M Technical Service for this information. In U.S. call 800-243-4630, in Canada call 800-267-4414

Duration of Protection | Depends on the contaminant, concentration of the contaminant, and the use conditions. Batteries provide up to 8 h service time (continuous air flow).

Recommended Use(s) | Rapid response. Designed to filter contaminants from ambient air and provide constant air flow to facepiece.

Physical Parameters

Sizes Available | One size
Weight | 10 lb
Package Size and Volume | 25.5 in x 15 in x 9.125 in

Power Requirements | Rechargeable battery with up to 8 h of service life per charge. Single-use lithium battery lasts up to 10 h with a 10 yr shelf life

Material Type	Neoprene facepiece. Nylon vest. Contact 3M Technical Service for full listing of parts and materials. In U.S. call 800–243–4630, in Canada call 800–267–4414
Construction Type	Not specified
Color	Black facepiece, belt, motor/blower, and battery.

Logistical Parameters

Ease of Use	PAPR is stored in a carrying bag that transforms into a vest with the PAPR system in place and ready for use; vest has belts and pockets for storage and support of gear Hook and loop fasteners make size adjustment quick and easy
Consumables	Battery, 8 h of service per charge. Lithium battery with up to 10 h service time. Various cartridges and filters available for a variety of response situations. Tested and authorized for purchase with the AP3 organic vapor/HEPA cartridge/filter under the CSEPP.
Maintenance Requirements	Inspection, replacement of worn parts. Fully charged battery (if using battery). See user instructions for details.
Shelf Life	Dependent on use conditions
Transportability	Easily transported
Operational Limitations	Not specified
Environmental Conditions	Contact 3M Technical Service for this information. In U.S. call 800–243–4630, in Canada call 800–267–4414
Unit Cost	$568
Maintenance Cost	Not specified
Warranty	Not specified
Don/Doff Information	Highly portable vest-mounted system is easy to put on and take off
Use/Reuse	Reusable
Launderability	Contact 3M Technical Service for this information. In U.S. call 800–243–4630, in Canada call 800–267–4414
Accessories	RRPAS System w/Breathe Easy 7 Facepiece, battery, and AP3 Organic Vapor/HEPA cartridge

Special Requirements

Training Requirements	Training required per OSHA 1910.134 and user instructions
Training Available	Yes
Manuals Available	User manual
Surveillance Testing Requirements	Preuse user inspection required each time before donning. Inspection following cleaning. Part replacement as necessary. Fit testing required before issue of equipment.
Support Equipment	Power unit works on either rechargeable or disposable lithium batteries with up to 8 h of service time. Cartridges and filters available for a variety of response situations.
Testing Information	Tested and authorized for purchase under the Chemical Stockpile Emergency Preparedness Program. Contact 3M Technical Service for this information. In U.S. call 800–243–4630, in Canada call 800–267–4414.
Applicable Regulations	NIOSH, OSHA 1910.134
Health Hazards	Products may contain latex. Contact 3M Technical Service for this information. In U.S. call 800–243–4630, in Canada call 800–267–4414.

Communications Interface Capability   Not specified

EOD Compatibility   Not specified

General

Name
ID# 52

Technology
PAPRs are motorized systems that use a filter to clean ambient air before it is delivered to the breathing zone of the user. A PAPR system typically includes a blower, battery, headpiece, and a breathing tube. Powered air unit provides high airflow; available for use with a wide range of hoods, helmets and facepieces. Breathe Easy™ system with the butyl rubber hood uses a rechargeable NiCad battery and an AEP3 organic vapor/acid gas/high efficiency cartridge.

Stock Number
260-10-21LRA01

Protection Type
Respiratory

Equipment Category
PAPR. The system provides continuous flow of filtered air to the wearer. The hood can be worn with facial hair and glasses and meets military standard MIL-C-51251A for resistance to chemical and biological weapons. The system is NIOSH-approved. The PAPR does not have a tight sealing surface around the face.

Availability
Commercially available

Current User(s)
Not specified

Manufacturer
3M
3M Center
Bldg. 235-2W-70
St. Paul, MN 55144-1000

Manufacturer Type
Domestic

Developer
3M

Source
3M
POC: Jean Koecher
651-736-8272 (Tel)

Certification
NIOSH-approved for certain organic vapors, acid gases and as a high efficiency filter when used with the AEP3 cartridge (4240-01-323-3530). Approval numbers available upon request. MIL-C-51251A for resistance to CB agents.

Operational Parameters

Chemical Warfare (CW) Agents Protected Against
Contact 3M Technical Service for this information. In U.S. call 800-243-4630, and in Canada call 800-267-4414.

Biological Warfare (BW) Agents Protected Against
Contact 3M Technical Service for this information. In U.S. call 800-243-4630, and in Canada call 800-267-4414.

Toxic Industrial Materials (TIMs) Protected Against
Contact 3M Technical Service for this information. In U.S. call 800-243-4630, and in Canada call 800-267-4414.

Duration of Protection	Depends on the contaminant, concentration of the contaminant, and the use conditions
Recommended Use(s)	Not specified
Physical Parameters	
Sizes Available	One size
Weight	8 lb
Package Size and Volume	17.2 in x 13.9 in x 6.9 in
Power Requirements	Rechargeable battery with up to 8 h of service life per charge. Single-use lithium battery lasts up to 10 h with a 10 yr shelf life
Material Type	Hood made of butyl rubber, which meets MIL–C–51251A. Contact 3M Technical Service for full listing of parts and materials. In U.S. call 800–243–4630, and in Canada call 800–267–4414.
Construction Type	Not specified
Color	Olive drab hood. Black belt and motor/blower.
Logistical Parameters	
Ease of Use	Power unit is belt-mounted for comfort
Consumables	Battery, 8 h of service per charge. Lithium battery with up to 10 h service time. System is NIOSH-approved with AEP3 (organic vapor/acid gas/HEPA) and AP3 (organic vapor/HEPA) cartridges and filters. Tested and authorized for purchase with the AP3 organic vapor/HEPA cartridge/filter under the CSEPP.
Maintenance Requirements	Inspection and replacement of worn parts. Fully charged battery (if using battery). See user instructions for details.
Shelf Life	Dependent on use conditions
Transportability	Easily transported
Operational Limitations	Not specified
Environmental Conditions	Contact 3M Technical Service for this information. In U.S. call 800–243–4630, and in Canada call 800–267–4414.
Unit Cost	$517
Maintenance Cost	Not specified
Warranty	Not specified
Don/Doff Information	None required
Use/Reuse	Reusable
Launderability	Contact 3M Technical Service for this information. In U.S. call 800–243–4630, and in Canada call 800–267–4414.
Accessories	Breathe Easy 10 with butyl rubber hood, lithium battery, and AP3 organic vapor/HEPA cartridge
Special Requirements	
Training Requirements	Training required per OSHA 1910.134 and user instructions
Training Available	Yes
Manuals Available	User manual
Surveillance Testing Requirements	Preuse user inspection required each time before donning. Inspection following cleaning. Part replacement as necessary. Fit testing required before issue of equipment.
Support Equipment	Cartridges (3) and battery charger.

Testing Information	ECBC–TR, January 2001. Contact 3M Technical Service for this information. In U.S. call 800–243–4630, and in Canada call 800–267–4414.
Applicable Regulations	OSHA 1910.134
Health Hazards	Products may contain latex. Contact 3M Technical Service for this information. In U.S. call 800–243–4630, and in Canada call 800–267–4414.
Communications Interface Capability	Not specified
EOD Compatibility	Not specified

General
Name
ID# 53

3M™ 5000 Series Full Facepiece Respirators

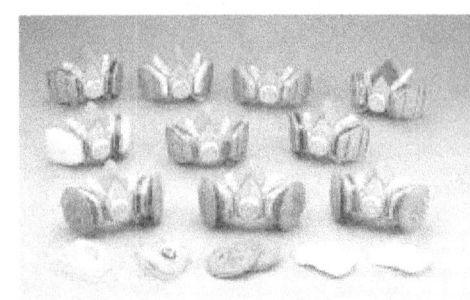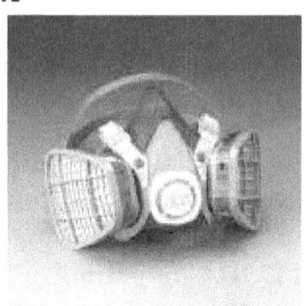

Technology
3M™ 5000 Series Maintenance-Free Gas and Vapor Respirators are dual cartridge half facepiece respirators. They can be used against a variety of gases and vapors according to their NIOSH approvals.

Stock Number
Product No.
Small: 51916
Medium: 52916
Large: 53916

Protection Type
Respiratory

Equipment Category
Respirator, elastomeric facepiece respirators, filters, and cartridges

Availability
Commercially available

Current User(s)
Not specified

Manufacturer
3M
3M Center
Bldg. 235-2W-70
St. Paul, MN 55144-1000

Manufacturer Type
Domestic

Developer
3M

Source
3M
POC: Jean Koecher
651-736-8272 (Tel)

Certification
NIOSH-approved for certain organic vapors, acid gases, ammonia/methylamine, formaldehyde, or hydrogen fluoride, and as a P100 particulate filter when used with the 60926 cartridge (4240-01-455-7370). Approval numbers available upon request.

Operational Parameters

Chemical Warfare (CW) Agents Protected Against
Contact 3M Technical Service for this information. In U.S. call 800-243-4630, and in Canada call 800-267-4414.

Biological Warfare (BW) Agents Protected Against
Contact 3M Technical Service for this information. In U.S. call 800-243-4630, and in Canada call 800-267-4414.

Toxic Industrial Materials (TIMs) Protected Against
Organic vapor, chlorine, hydrogen chloride, chlorine dioxide, sulfur dioxide, hydrogen sulfide (escape only), ammonia/methylamine, or hydrogen fluoride cartridge with P100 particulate filter

Duration of Protection
Depends on the contaminant, concentration of the contaminant, and the use conditions

Recommended Use(s)
Not specified

Physical Parameters

Sizes Available
Small, medium, and large

Weight
1.2 lb

Package Size and Volume
16.7 in x 12.5 in x 10.7 in

Power Requirements	None (when used in air purifying mode)
Material Type	Silicone face seal. Contact 3M Technical Service for listing of parts and materials. In U.S. call 800–243–4630, and in Canada call 800–267–4414.
Construction Type	Not specified
Color	Black facepiece

Logistical Parameters

Ease of Use	Lightweight facepiece is comfortable for extended use
Consumables	60929 cartridges, P100 particulate filters
Maintenance Requirements	Inspection and replacement of worn parts. See user instructions for details.
Shelf Life	Dependent on use conditions
Transportability	Easily transported
Operational Limitations	Not specified
Environmental Conditions	Contact 3M Technical Service for this information. In U.S. call 800–243–4630, and in Canada call 800–267–4414.
Unit Cost	$267
Maintenance Cost	Not specified
Warranty	Not specified
Don/Doff Information	None required
Use/Reuse	Reusable
Launderability	Contact 3M Technical Service for this information. In U.S. call 800–243–4630, and in Canada call 800–267–4414.
Accessories	Not specified

Special Requirements

Training Requirements	Training required per OSHA 1910.134 and user instructions
Training Available	Yes
Manuals Available	User manual
Surveillance Testing Requirements	Preuse user inspection required each time before donning. Inspection following cleaning. Part replacement as necessary. Fit testing required before issue of equipment.
Support Equipment	Cartridges (2)
Testing Information	Contact 3M Technical Service for this information. In U.S. call 800–243–4630, and in Canada call 800–267–4414.
Applicable Regulations	OSHA 1910.134
Health Hazards	Products may contain latex. Contact 3M Technical Service for this information. In U.S. call 800–243–4630, and in Canada call 800–267–4414.
Communications Interface Capability	Not specified
EOD Compatibility	Not specified

General

Name
ID# 54

3M™ 6000 Series Full Facepiece Respirator

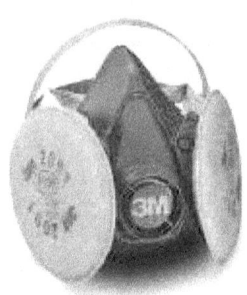 

Technology

3M™ 6000 Series facepieces are half and full facepiece elastomeric type. They are designed for comfort, convenience, and economy. The reusable facepieces are made of a soft, comfortable material and can be adjusted for individual fitting.

Stock Number

4240-01-454-8535

Protection Type

Respiratory

Equipment Category

Respirator, elastomeric facepiece respirators, filters, and cartridges. 3M™ 6000 Series respirator facepieces, cartridges, filters, assemblies and accessories provide an easy-to-use, comfortable and economical way to fulfill the requirements of a respiratory protection program.

Availability

Commercially available

Current User(s)

Not specified

Manufacturer

3M
3M Center
Bldg. 235-2W-70
St. Paul, MN 55144-1000

Manufacturer Type

Domestic

Developer

3M

Source

3M
POC: Jean Koecher
651-736-8272 (Tel)

Certification

NIOSH-approved for certain organic vapors, acid gases, ammonia/methylamine, formaldehyde, or hydrogen fluoride, and as a P100 particulate filter when used with the 60926 cartridge (4240-01-455-7370). Approval numbers available upon request.

Operational Parameters

Chemical Warfare (CW) Agents Protected Against

Contact 3M Technical Service for this information. In U.S. call 800-243-4630, and in Canada call 800-267-4414.

Biological Warfare (BW) Agents Protected Against

Contact 3M Technical Service for this information. In U.S. call 800-243-4630, and in Canada call 800-267-4414.

Toxic Industrial Materials (TIMs) Protected Against

Ammonia, chlorine, hydrogen chloride, hydrogen fluoride, hydrogen sulfide, and sulfur dioxide

Duration of Protection

Depends on the contaminant, concentration of the contaminant, and the use conditions

Recommended Use(s)

Not specified

Physical Parameters

Sizes Available

Small, medium, and large

Weight

1.2 lb

Package Size and Volume	16.7 in x 12.5 in x 10.7 in
Power Requirements	None (when used in air purifying mode)
Material Type	Silicone face seal. Contact 3M Technical Service for listing of parts and materials. In U.S. call 00–243–4630, and in Canada call 800–267–4414.
Construction Type	Not specified
Color	Black facepiece
Logistical Parameters	
Ease of Use	Lightweight facepiece is comfortable for extended use
Consumables	60929 cartridges and P100 particulate filters
Maintenance Requirements	Inspection and replacement of worn parts. See user instructions for details.
Shelf Life	Dependent on use conditions
Transportability	Easily transported
Operational Limitations	Not specified
Environmental Conditions	Contact 3M Technical Service for this information. In U.S. call 800–243–4630, and in Canada call 800–267–4414.
Unit Cost	$267
Maintenance Cost	Not specified
Warranty	Not specified
Don/Doff Information	None required
Use/Reuse	Reusable
Launderability	Contact 3M Technical Service for this information. In U.S. call 800–243–4630, and in Canada call 800–267–4414.
Accessories	Not specified
Special Requirements	
Training Requirements	Training required per OSHA 1910.134 and user instructions
Training Available	Yes
Manuals Available	User manual
Surveillance Testing Requirements	Preuse user inspection required each time before donning. Inspection following cleaning. Part replacement as necessary. Fit testing required before issue of equipment.
Support Equipment	Cartridges (2)
Testing Information	Contact 3M Technical Service for this information. In U.S. call 800–243–4630, and in Canada call 800–267–4414.
Applicable Regulations	OSHA 1910.134
Health Hazards	Products may contain latex. Contact 3M Technical Service for this information. In U.S. call 800–243–4630, and in Canada call 800–267–4414.
Communications Interface Capability	Not specified
EOD Compatibility	Not specified

General

Name
ID# 55

3M™ 7800S-BA Full Facepiece Respirators

Technology

3M™ 7000 Series respirator facepieces, cartridges, filters, accessories and quantitative fit test equipment are used to fulfill the requirements of a respirator protection program.
3M™ 7800S-BA full facepiece respirators are designed specifically for use with 3M™ SCBA. They can be used with 3M™ Escort™, SCBAG™ and 2000 Series SCBA Systems.

Stock Number
Not specified

Protection Type
Respiratory and full facepiece

Equipment Category
Respirator, negative-pressure, elastomeric facepiece respirators, filters, and cartridges

Availability
Not specified

Current User(s)
Not specified

Manufacturer
3M
3M Center
Bldg. 235-2W-70
St. Paul, MN 55144-1000

Manufacturer Type
Domestic

Developer
3M

Source
3M
POC: Jean Koecher
651-736-8272 (Tel)

Certification
Not specified

Operational Parameters

Chemical Warfare (CW) Agents Protected Against
Not specified

Biological Warfare (BW) Agents Protected Against
Not specified

Toxic Industrial Materials (TIMs) Protected Against
Used against organic vapors, acid gases, ammonia, methylamine, formaldehyde and particles

Duration of Protection
Not specified

Recommended Use(s)
Not specified

Physical Parameters

Sizes Available
Facemask: small, medium, and large
Waist belt: adjustable to fit most sizes

Weight
Not specified

Package Size and Volume
Not specified

Power Requirements
Not specified

Material Type	These facepieces are made of a soft, comfortable silicone. Waist belt, along with the belt clip assembly, holds the supplied air hose in place. It is made of a black vinyl material to resist contaminants.
Construction Type	Not specified
Color	Not specified

Logistical Parameters

Ease of Use	Not specified
Consumables	Not specified
Maintenance Requirements	Not specified
Shelf Life	Not specified
Transportability	Not specified
Operational Limitations	Not specified
Environmental Conditions	Not specified
Unit Cost	Not specified
Maintenance Cost	Not specified
Warranty	Not specified
Don/Doff Information	Not specified
Use/Reuse	Not specified
Launderability	Not specified
Accessories	Parts include head and neck strap assemblies, eyeglass frame and mount, spectacle kit, auto-darkening lens (shades 9–12), tinted lens cover, welder's face shield (auto-darkening), welder's face shield kit, belt clip assembly, breathing tube, shoulder strap, and high pressure type supplied air hoses. Valve kits include vinyl waist belt, vinyl shoulder strap, two position exhalation valve assembly, pressure demand valve assembly, breathing tube, belt clip assembly, pressure demand adapter, and facepiece plug.

Special Requirements

Training Requirements	Not specified
Training Available	Not specified
Manuals Available	Not specified
Surveillance Testing Requirements	Not specified
Support Equipment	Pressure demand systems facepieces. Replacement parts include waist belt, shoulder strap, exhalation valve, pressure demand valve, pressure demand adapter, belt clip assembly, O-rings, seals and pressure demand springs.
Testing Information	Not specified
Applicable Regulations	Not specified
Health Hazards	Do not use under the following conditions: While performing or observing abrasive blasting (sandblasting) operations, for fire fighting, in any atmosphere having less than the equivalent of 19.5 % oxygen by volume at sea level, and in poorly ventilated areas.
Communications Interface Capability	Not specified
EOD Compatibility	Not specified

General
Name
ID# 56

3M™ SCBAG Self-Contained Breathing Apparatus

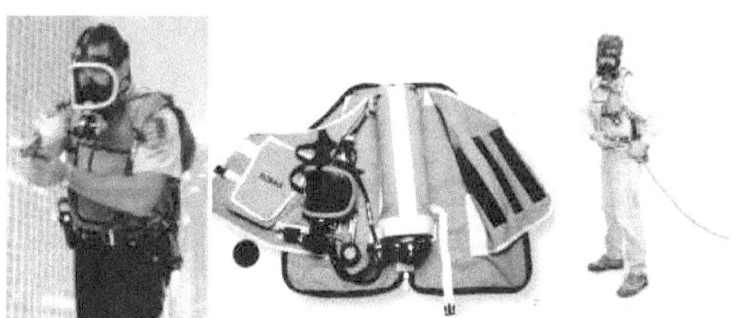

Technology

Pressure-demand SCBA. For use in (IDLH) environments such as oxygen deficient and containing CB agents. Thirty (30) min SCBA is stored in a unique carrying bag that opens to form a vest with the SCBA system in place and ready for use. For use in environments that are IDLH such as oxygen deficient atmospheres and those containing chemical and biological agents; available with or without airline connection; and the highest level of respiratory protection available.

Stock Number
4240–01–418–2633

Protection Type
Respiratory

Equipment Category
SCBA, pressure demand

Availability
Commercially available

Current User(s)
Not specified

Manufacturer
3M
3M Center
Bldg. 235–2W–70
St. Paul, MN 55144–1000

Manufacturer Type
Domestic

Developer
3M

Source
3M
POC: Jean Koecher
651–736–8272 (Tel)

Certification
NIOSH-approved in several configurations. Approval numbers available upon request.

Operational Parameters

Chemical Warfare (CW) Agents Protected Against

For use in environments that are IDLH such as oxygen deficient atmospheres and those containing chemical and biological agents. Contact 3M Technical Service for this information. In U.S. call 800–243–4630, and in Canada call 800–267–4414 .

Biological Warfare (BW) Agents Protected Against

For use in environments that are IDLH such as oxygen deficient atmospheres and those containing chemical and biological agents. Contact 3M Technical Service for this information. In U.S. call 800–243–4630, and in Canada call 800–267–4414.

Toxic Industrial Materials (TIMs) Protected Against

For use in environments that are IDLH such as oxygen deficient atmospheres and those containing chemical and biological agents. Contact 3M Technical Service for this information. In U.S. call 800–243–4630, and in Canada call 800–267–4414.

Duration of Protection	30 min SCBA. Depends on the contaminant, concentration of the contaminant, and the use conditions.
Recommended Use(s)	For use in environments that are IDLH

Physical Parameters

Sizes Available	One size
Weight	System weighs maximum of 22.1 lb with a 4500 psi, and 30 min cylinder
Package Size and Volume	26 in x 8 in x 16 in
Power Requirements	Supplied air line, 85psig to 125 psig, or fully charged cylinder
Material Type	Vest/bag is made of durable, abrasion resistant fabric for long use; silicone facepiece has integral speaking diaphragm and nose cup, nylon harness, and aluminum cylinder. Contact 3M Technical Service for full listing of parts and materials. In U.S. call 800–243–4630, and in Canada call 800–267–4414.
Construction Type	Hook and loop fasteners make size adjustment very fast and easy
Color	Black facepiece with brown and black optional vest and yellow cylinder

Logistical Parameters

Ease of Use	Stored in a unique carrying bag that opens to form a vest with the SCBA system in place and ready for use. Ready and available when and where you need it.
Consumables	NIOSH-approved air cylinders
Maintenance Requirements	Inspection, replacement of worn parts, fully charged cylinder. Yearly system check, and 3 yr overhaul. See user instructions for details.
Shelf Life	Dependent on use conditions
Transportability	Easily transported
Operational Limitations	Not specified
Environmental Conditions	Contact 3M Technical Service for this information. In U.S. call 800–243–4630, and in Canada call 800–267–4414.
Unit Cost	$1.2K
Maintenance Cost	Not specified
Warranty	Not specified
Don/Doff Information	Unique carrying bag that opens to form a vest with the SCBA system in place and ready for use. Ready and available when and where you need it.
Use/Reuse	Reusable
Launderability	Contact 3M Technical Service for this information. In U.S. call 800–243–4630, and in Canada call 800–267–4414.
Accessories	SCBAG system, hoop-wrapped 4500 psi cylinder, and PBI/Kevlar vest. Available with or without airline connection; easy to read low pressure gauge.

Special Requirements

Training Requirements	Training required per OSHA 1910.134 and User Instructions
Training Available	Yes
Manuals Available	User manual
Surveillance Testing Requirements	Preuse user inspection required each time before donning. Inspection following cleaning. Monthly inspection required. Part replacement as necessary. Fit testing required before issue of equipment.
Support Equipment	Airline optional

Testing Information	Contact 3M Technical Service for this information. In U.S. call 800–243–4630, and in Canada call 800–267–4414.
Applicable Regulations	NIOSH-approved; OSHA 1910.134
Health Hazards	Products may contain latex. Contact 3M Technical Service for this information. In U.S. call 800–243–4630, and in Canada call 800–267–4414.
Communications Interface Capability	Not specified
EOD Compatibility	Not specified

General
Name
ID# 57

3M™ Belt-Mounted PAPR

Technology

PAPRs are motorized systems that use a filter to clean ambient air before it is delivered to the breathing zone of the user. A PAPR system typically includes a blower, battery, headpiece, and a breathing tube. Powered air unit provides high airflow; available for use with a wide range of hoods, helmets and facepieces.

Stock Number

Not specified

Protection Type

Respiratory

Equipment Category

PAPR, belt mounted

Availability

Not specified

Current User(s)

Not specified

Manufacturer

3M
3M Center
Bldg. 235-2W-70
St. Paul, MN 55144-1000

Manufacturer Type

Domestic

Developer

3M

Source

3M
POC: Jean Koecher
651-736-8272 (Tel)

Certification

NIOSH-approved

Operational Parameters
Chemical Warfare (CW) Agents Protected Against

Not specified

Biological Warfare (BW) Agents Protected Against

Not specified

Toxic Industrial Materials (TIMs) Protected Against

Not specified

Duration of Protection

Not specified

Recommended Use(s)

Provides cartridge and filter options for a wide variety of first response uses

Physical Parameters
Sizes Available

Not specified

Weight

Approximate system weight: 7.1 lb

Package Size and Volume

Complete power system contours to hip and body for complete comfort

Power Requirements

Battery provides up to 8 h of service per charge

Material Type

7800S silicone facepiece

Construction Type	Not specified
Color	Not specified

Logistical Parameters

Ease of Use	Complete power system contours to hip and body for complete comfort
Consumables	Not specified
Maintenance Requirements	Not specified
Shelf Life	Not specified
Transportability	Easily transported
Operational Limitations	Not specified
Environmental Conditions	Not specified
Unit Cost	Not specified
Maintenance Cost	Not specified
Warranty	Not specified
Don/Doff Information	Vinyl waist belt and optional shoulder strap are durable and easy to decontaminate
Use/Reuse	Not specified
Launderability	Vinyl waist belt and optional shoulder strap are durable and easy to decontaminate
Accessories	System Components: 7800S silicone facepiece, breathing tube, motor blower, power cord, battery pack, battery charger, flow meter, blower plugs, filter plugs, and web belt

Special Requirements

Training Requirements	Not specified
Training Available	Not specified
Manuals Available	Not specified
Surveillance Testing Requirements	Not specified
Support Equipment	See accessories
Testing Information	Not specified
Applicable Regulations	Not specified
Health Hazards	Not specified
Communications Interface Capability	Not specified
EOD Compatibility	Not specified

General

Name
ID# 58

3M™ GVP Belt-Mounted Powered Air Purifying Respirator

Technology

3M™ Belt-Mounted GVP-Series Powered Air Purifying Respirators (PAPRs) provide high-level protection and exceptional performance. These systems are available with helmets, hoods, head cover, loose-fitting facepieces, and tight-fitting facepieces.

Stock Number
4240–01–395–9180

Protection Type
Respiratory

Equipment Category
PAPR, belt mounted, and powered

Availability
Commercially available

Current User(s)
Not specified

Manufacturer
3M
3M Center
Bldg. 235–2W–70
St. Paul, MN 55144–1000

Manufacturer Type
Domestic

Developer
3M

Source
3M
POC: Jean Koecher
651–736–8272 (Tel)

Certification
NIOSH-approved for certain organic vapors, acid gases and as a high efficiency filter when used with the GVP–443 cartridge (4240–01–394–6336). Approval numbers available upon request.

Operational Parameters

Chemical Warfare (CW) Agents Protected Against
Contact 3M Technical Service for this information. In U.S. call 800–243–4630, and in Canada call 800–267–4414.

Biological Warfare (BW) Agents Protected Against
Contact 3M Technical Service for this information. In U.S. call 800–243–4630, and in Canada call 800–267–4414.

Toxic Industrial Materials (TIMs) Protected Against
3M™ GVP-Series cartridges and filters attach to the PAPR unit filter a wide variety of acid gases, organic vapors, formaldehyde, ammonia, and particles. Contact 3M Technical Service for this information. In U.S. call 800–243–4630, and in Canada call 800–267–4414.

Duration of Protection
Depends on the contaminant, concentration of the contaminant, and the use conditions

Recommended Use(s)
Not specified

Physical Parameters

Sizes Available
Small, medium, and large

Weight
7.1 lb

Package Size and Volume
12.4 in x 8.4 in x 8.6 in

Power Requirements
Rechargeable battery with up to 8 h of service life per charge

Material Type	Depends on exact system selected. Contact 3M Technical Service for listing of parts and materials. In U.S. call 800–243–4630, and in Canada call 800–267–4414.
Construction Type	Not specified
Color	Black facepiece, belt, motor/blower, and battery

Logistical Parameters

Ease of Use	The complete power system contours to hip and body for maximum comfort
Consumables	Battery (8 h of service per charge), and 3M™ GVP-Series filters
Maintenance Requirements	Inspection and replacement of worn parts. Fully charged battery. See User Instructions for details.
Shelf Life	Dependent on use conditions
Transportability	Easily transported
Operational Limitations	Not specified
Environmental Conditions	Contact 3M Technical Service for this information. In U.S. call 800–243–4630, and in Canada call 800–267–4414.
Unit Cost	$399
Maintenance Cost	Not specified
Warranty	Not specified
Don/Doff Information	None required
Use/Reuse	Reusable
Launderability	Contact 3M Technical Service for this information. In U.S. call 800–243–4630, and in Canada call 800–267–4414.
Accessories	Belt-mounted PAPR assembly; including motor blower, power cord, battery pack, battery charger, flow meter, blower plugs, and web belt

Special Requirements

Training Requirements	Training required per OSHA 1910.134 and User Instructions
Training Available	Yes
Manuals Available	User manual
Surveillance Testing Requirements	Preuse user inspection required each time before donning. Inspection following cleaning. Part replacement as necessary. Fit testing required before issue of equipment.
Support Equipment	Cartridge and battery
Testing Information	Contact 3M Technical Service for this information. In U.S. call 800–243–4630, and in Canada call 800–267–4414.
Applicable Regulations	OSHA 1910.134
Health Hazards	Products may contain latex. Contact 3M Technical Service for this information. In U.S. call 800–243–4630, and in Canada call 800–267–4414.
Communications Interface Capability	Not specified
EOD Compatibility	Not specified

General

Name
ID# 59

3M™ Escort Combination ESCBA/Supplied Air Respirator

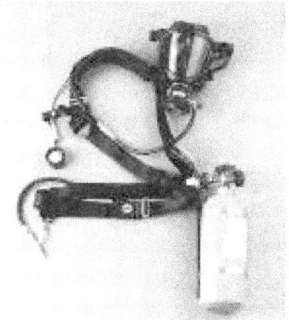

Technology

3M™ Escort™ Combination ESCBA/Supplied Air Respirator Products include the 3M™ 7800S-BA Full Facepiece (available in three sizes) with pressure demand valve, 5 min or 15 min cylinders, and nylon harness

Stock Number — BA-3005-L

Protection Type — Respiratory

Equipment Category — Respirator, combination ESCBA, and supplied air

Availability — Commercially available

Current User(s) — Not specified

Manufacturer
3M
3M Center
Bldg. 235-2W-70
St. Paul, MN 55144-1000

Manufacturer Type — Domestic

Developer — 3M

Source
3M
POC: Jean Koecher
651-736-8272 (Tel)

Certification — NIOSH-approved in several configurations. Approval numbers available upon request.

Operational Parameters

Chemical Warfare (CW) Agents Protected Against — Contact 3M Technical Service for this information. In U.S. call 800-243-4630, and in Canada call 800-267-4414.

Biological Warfare (BW) Agents Protected Against — Contact 3M Technical Service for this information. In U.S. call 800-243-4630, and in Canada call 800-267-4414.

Toxic Industrial Materials (TIMs) Protected Against — Contact 3M Technical Service for this information. In U.S. call 800-243-4630, and in Canada call 800-267-4414.

Duration of Protection — Depends on the contaminant, concentration of the contaminant, and the use conditions

Recommended Use(s) — Not specified

Physical Parameters

Sizes Available — One size

Weight — 5.3 lb

Package Size and Volume — 17.2 in x 13.9 in x 6.9 in

Power Requirements — Supplied air line, 85 psig to 25 psig, or fully charged cylinder

Material Type — Silicone facepiece, nylon harness, and aluminum cylinder. Contact 3M Technical Service for full listing of parts and materials. In U.S. call 800-243-4630, and in Canada call 800-267-4414.

Construction Type — Not specified

Color	Black facepiece and belt. Yellow escape cylinder.

Logistical Parameters

Ease of Use	Lightweight system, and belt-mounted for comfort
Consumables	NIOSH-approved air cylinders
Maintenance Requirements	Inspection, replacement of worn parts, and fully charged cylinder. Yearly system check, 3 yr overhaul. See user instructions for details.
Shelf Life	Dependent on use conditions
Transportability	Easily transported
Operational Limitations	Not specified
Environmental Conditions	Contact 3M Technical Service for this information. In U.S. call 800–243–4630, and in Canada call 800–267–4414.
Unit Cost	$712
Maintenance Cost	Not specified
Warranty	Not specified
Don/Doff Information	None required
Use/Reuse	Reusable
Launderability	Contact 3M Technical Service for this information. In U.S. call 800–243–4630, and in Canada call 800–267–4414.
Accessories	Aluminum cylinder (5 min, 2216 psi) and valve, hoop wrapped cylinder (15 min, 3000 psi) and valve, and a wide selection of airline hoses

Special Requirements

Training Requirements	Training required per OSHA 1910.134 and User Instructions
Training Available	Yes
Manuals Available	User manual
Surveillance Testing Requirements	Preuse user inspection required each time before donning. Inspection following cleaning. Monthly inspection required. Part replacement as necessary. Fit testing required before issue of equipment.
Support Equipment	Airline
Testing Information	Contact 3M Technical Service for this information. In U.S. call 800–243–4630, and in Canada call 800–267–4414.
Applicable Regulations	OSHA 1910.134
Health Hazards	Products may contain latex. Contact 3M Technical Service for this information. In U.S. call 800–243–4630, and in Canada call 800–267–4414.
Communications Interface Capability	Not specified
EOD Compatibility	Not specified

General

Name

ID# 60

3M™ Full Facepiece FR-M40, military-style (replaced #54 SGE 400)

Technology

Military-style respirator system, designed for emergency response situations. The 3M™ Full Facepiece FR-M40 is made of a soft, conformable silicone material with a single flanged edge for a secure seal. The 3M Cartridge FR-C2A1 can be mounted on either side of the facepiece and a drinking tube can be used without removing the facepiece. Eyepiece outserts protect the primary lens against scratches. An optional butyl rubber second skin and hood fit over the facepiece to help protect it from industrial chemicals or chemical warfare agents.

Stock Number

Not specified

Protection Type

Respiratory

Equipment Category

Respirator, full facepiece military-style, full facepiece respirator system featuring a cartridge with proven carbon filtering capabilities

Availability

November 2000

Current User(s)

Not specified

Manufacturer

3M
3M Center
Bldg. 235-2W-70
St. Paul, MN 55144-1000

Manufacturer Type

Domestic

Developer

3M

Source

3M OH and ESD
P.O. Box 33275
St. Paul, MN 55133-3275
POC: Jean Koecher
651-736-8272 (Tel)

Certification

NIOSH
The cartridge is manufactured in accordance with U.S. MIL-C 51560(EA) and EA-C-1704 for chemical warfare agents

Operational Parameters

Chemical Warfare (CW) Agents Protected Against

It has been tested to military specifications to filter a wide range of certain chemical warfare agents such as nerve agents, tear agents, blood agents, as well as chlorine, phosgene, chloropicrin and diphenylchloroarsine

Biological Warfare (BW) Agents Protected Against

Not specified

Toxic Industrial Materials (TIMs) Protected Against

Chlorine, hydrogen chloride, sulfur dioxide, hydrogen sulfide, hydrogen fluoride, ammonia, and formaldehyde

Duration of Protection	Not specified
Recommended Use(s)	This system is designed to meet the performance requirements of law enforcement agencies, security personnel, medical personnel, HAZMAT teams, emergency response technicians (EMTs), and domestic preparedness personnel

Physical Parameters

Sizes Available	Not specified
Weight	Not specified
Package Size and Volume	Not specified
Power Requirements	Not specified
Material Type	Facepiece is conformable silicone material with a single flanged edge for a secure seal. An optional butyl rubber second skin and hood fit over the facepiece to help protect it from industrial chemicals or chemical warfare agents.
Construction Type	Not specified
Color	Not specified

Logistical Parameters

Ease of Use	Not specified
Consumables	Not specified
Maintenance Requirements	Not specified
Shelf Life	Not specified
Transportability	Not specified
Operational Limitations	Not specified
Environmental Conditions	Not specified
Unit Cost	Not specified
Maintenance Cost	Not specified
Warranty	Not specified
Don/Doff Information	Not specified
Use/Reuse	Not specified
Launderability	Not specified
Accessories	3M Cartridge FR–C2A1 can be mounted on either side of the facepiece and a drinking tube can be used without removing the facepiece. Eyepiece outserts protect the primary lens against scratches. An optional butyl rubber second skin and hood fit over the facepiece to help protect it from industrial chemicals or chemical warfare agents.

Special Requirements

Training Requirements	Not specified
Training Available	Not specified
Manuals Available	Not specified
Surveillance Testing Requirements	Not specified
Support Equipment	Not specified
Testing Information	Not specified

Applicable Regulations   NIOSH-approved for use against certain acid gases, CN, CS and as a P100 particulate filter. The cartridge is manufactured in accordance with U. S. MIL−C51560(EA) and EA−C−1704 for chemical warfare agents.

Health Hazards   Not specified

Communications Interface Capability   Not specified

EOD Compatibility   Not specified

General

Name
ID# 61

Scott AV 2000 AV-2000® Facepiece

Technology

The advanced AV-2000 facepiece gives new meaning to the term flexibility. It is designed to be interchangeable with the Scott full line of SCBA, air-supplied and air-purifying respirators as well as the complete line of communications products. The AV-2000 minimizes equipment inventories and simplifies user training. This state-of-the-art facepiece is the key to a wide range of Scott products.

Stock Number — Not specified

Protection Type — Respiratory

Equipment Category — Facepiece, designed to be interchangeable with SCBA, air-supplied and air-purifying respirators

Availability — Not specified

Current User(s) — Not specified

Manufacturer — Scott Health and Safety

Manufacturer Type — Domestic

Developer — Scott Health and Safety

Source — Lifecycle Plan SNL-795, September 30, 1998

Certification — Not specified

Operational Parameters

Chemical Warfare (CW) Agents Protected Against — Not specified

Biological Warfare (BW) Agents Protected Against — Not specified

Toxic Industrial Materials (TIMs) Protected Against — Not specified

Duration of Protection — Not specified

Recommended Use(s) — Not specified

Physical Parameters

Sizes Available — Not specified

Weight — Not specified

Package Size and Volume — Not specified

Power Requirements — Not specified

Material Type — Not specified

Construction Type — Not specified

Color — Not specified

Logistical Parameters

Ease of Use	Not specified
Consumables	Not specified
Maintenance Requirements	Not specified
Shelf Life	Not specified
Transportability	Not specified
Operational Limitations	Not specified
Environmental Conditions	Not specified
Unit Cost	Not specified
Maintenance Cost	Not specified
Warranty	Not specified
Don/Doff Information	Not specified
Use/Reuse	Not specified
Launderability	Not specified
Accessories	Not specified

Special Requirements

Training Requirements	Not specified
Training Available	Not specified
Manuals Available	Not specified
Surveillance Testing Requirements	Not specified
Support Equipment	Not specified
Testing Information	Not specified
Applicable Regulations	Not specified
Health Hazards	Not specified
Communications Interface Capability	It is designed to be compatible with a complete line of communications products
EOD Compatibility	Not specified

General

Name
ID# 62

Scott C420 Variflo™ PAPR

Technology	PAPR Connects to AV 2000 by 40 mm adapter
Stock Number	Not specified
Protection Type	Respiratory
Equipment Category	PAPR
Availability	Commercial
Current User(s)	U.S. Military and NATO
Manufacturer	Scott Health and Safety
Manufacturer Type	Domestic
Developer	Scott Health and Safety
Source	Scott Health and Safety Slides
Certification	NFPA, OSHA, NIOSH, and DOJ Foundation

Operational Parameters

Chemical Warfare (CW) Agents Protected Against	Not specified
Biological Warfare (BW) Agents Protected Against	Not specified
Toxic Industrial Materials (TIMs) Protected Against	Not specified
Duration of Protection	Not specified
Recommended Use(s)	HAZMAT, Utility Companies, Hospitals, SWAT, airports, DOE, DOJ, ATF, DOT, and public arena security

Physical Parameters

Sizes Available	Not specified
Weight	Not specified
Package Size and Volume	Not specified
Power Requirements	Battery and motor
Material Type	Not specified
Construction Type	Not specified
Color	Not specified

Logistical Parameters

Ease of Use	Not specified
Consumables	Uses existing NBC cans C2A1/HEPA/P100

Maintenance Requirements	Not specified
Shelf Life	Not specified
Transportability	Not specified
Operational Limitations	Ideal for long work periods of detection or decontamination. Supports wearers who have Pulmonary challenges; provides limited relief in warm and hot weather.
Environmental Conditions	Not specified
Unit Cost	Not specified
Maintenance Cost	Not specified
Warranty	Not specified
Don/Doff Information	Not specified
Use/Reuse	Not specified
Launderability	Not specified
Accessories	Facepiece

Special Requirements

Training Requirements	Not specified
Training Available	Not specified
Manuals Available	Not specified
Surveillance Testing Requirements	Not specified
Support Equipment	Filters
Testing Information	Not specified
Applicable Regulations	Not specified
Health Hazards	Not specified
Communications Interface Capability	EZ Radio, Envoy radioxon, Con Space Link, voice amplifier, and enhancements
EOD Compatibility	Not specified

General
Name
ID# 63

PAN1 Dual Cartridge Full Face Respirator

Technology

Dual cartridge negative pressure respirator. Panoramic respirators are outstandingly effective, combining excellent protection with superior comfort. The latest in materials technology and innovative engineering has successfully industrialized a proven military design into a lightweight, ergonomically correct facepiece with a soft, comfortable, yet firm fit. Respirator; dual cartridge negative pressure respirator.

Stock Number

PAN1

Protection Type

Respiratory

Equipment Category

Respirator and dual cartridge negative pressure

Availability

Commercial

Current User(s)

Safety market

Manufacturer

Shalon Chemical Industries Ltd.
25, Nahmani St.
Tel-Aviv 65794, Israel
Kenneth Samet, Quality Assurance Manager
972–8–6879111 (Tel)
972–8–6811115 (Fax)

U.S. Distribution:
Sellstrom Manufacturing Co.
Palatine, IL 60067
847–358–2000 (Tel)
847–358–8564 (Fax)

Neoterik Health Tech. Inc.
Woodsboro, MD 21798
301–845–2777 (Tel)
301–845–2213 (Fax)

Manufacturer Type

Foreign

Developer

Shalon Chemical Industries

Source

Internet: www.doryanet.co.il/Shalon/23.htm
www.shalon.co.il
shalon@shalon.co.il

Certification

NIOSH

Operational Parameters
Chemical Warfare (CW) Agents Protected Against

Protection provided is dependent on the type of filter cartridges that are used (see accessories)

Biological Warfare (BW) Agents Protected Against	Protection provided is dependent on the type of filter cartridges that are used (see accessories)
Toxic Industrial Materials (TIMs) Protected Against	Protection provided is dependent on the type of filter cartridges that are used (see accessories)
Duration of Protection	Not specified
Recommended Use(s)	Civil defense, industrial, and safety market

Physical Parameters

Sizes Available	One size fits all
Weight	Lightweight with effective lasting protection for extended duration wear
Package Size and Volume	Cardboard box, 11 1/4 in x 6 1/4 in x 6 in
Power Requirements	Not applicable
Material Type	Specially formulated rubber material combining superior chemical permeation resistance and durability, with smooth soft feel. Also available with silicone facepiece.
Construction Type	Integral nose-cup with controlled air flow; highly elasticized head harness; and facepiece support
Color	Black (blue and yellow available in silicone)

Logistical Parameters

Ease of Use	Lightweight and ergonomically correct facepiece. Highly elasticized head harness with quick-release buckles with rollers for easy donning, simple adjustment and fast removal.
Consumables	Filters
Maintenance Requirements	Not specified
Shelf Life	Not specified
Transportability	Easily transportable
Operational Limitations	Not specified
Environmental Conditions	Normal environments
Unit Cost	Less than $150
Maintenance Cost	Not specified
Warranty	Not specified
Don/Doff Information	Highly elasticized head harness with quick-release buckles with rollers for easy donning, simple adjustment and fast removal
Use/Reuse	Not specified
Launderability	Can be cleaned and reused many times
Accessories	Types of cartridges availabale: OV, AG, OV/AG, AM/MA, P100, N95, OV–P100, AG–P100, OV/AG–P100, and AM/MA–P100

Special Requirements

Training Requirements	Little training required
Training Available	Not specified
Manuals Available	User manual
Surveillance Testing Requirements	Not specified
Support Equipment	Not applicable
Testing Information	Not specified
Applicable Regulations	Not specified
Health Hazards	Not specified

**Communications Interface
Capability**

Speaking diaphragm for clear voice communication.

EOD Compatibility

Not specified

General

Name
ID# 64

PAN2 Single Filter Canister

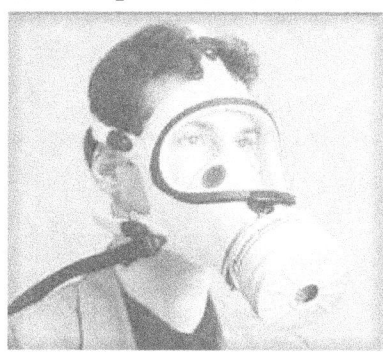

Technology

Canister type with standard 40 mm threaded connection for single filter canister. Panoramic respirators are outstandingly effective, combining excellent protection with superior comfort. The latest in materials technology and innovative engineering has successfully industrialized a proven military design into a lightweight, ergonomically correct facepiece with a soft, comfortable, yet firm fit. Respirator; single canister type respirator with standard 40 mm threaded connection.

Stock Number

PAN2

Protection Type

Respiratory

Equipment Category

Respirator/single canister type respirator with standard connection

Availability

Commercial

Current User(s)

Safety market and several police forces

Manufacturer

Shalon Chemical Industries Ltd.
25, Nahmani St.
Tel-Aviv 65794, Israel
POC: Kenneth Samet, Quality Assurance Manager
972-8-6879111 (Tel)
972-8-6811115 (Fax)

U.S. Distribution:
Sellstrom Manufacturing Co.
Palatine, IL 60067
847-358-2000 (Tel)
847-358-8564 (Fax)

Neoterik Health Tech. Inc.
Woodsboro, MD 21798
301-845-2777 (Tel)
301-845-2213 (Fax)

Manufacturer Type

Foreign

Developer

Shalon Chemical Industries

Source

Internet: www.doryanet.co.il/Shalon/23.htm
www.shalon.co.il
shalon@shalon.co.il

Certification

EN-136 approved respirator

Operational Parameters

Chemical Warfare (CW)
Agents Protected Against

Protection provided is dependent on the type of filter canister that is used (see accessories)

Biological Warfare (BW) Agents Protected Against	Not specified
Toxic Industrial Materials (TIMs) Protected Against	Not specified
Duration of Protection	Not specified
Recommended Use(s)	Civil defense, military, police, and industrial safety

Physical Parameters

Sizes Available	One size fits all
Weight	Lightweight with effective lasting protection for extended duration wear
Package Size and Volume	Cardboard box, 11 1/4 in x 6 1/4 in x 6 in
Power Requirements	Not applicable
Material Type	Specially formulated rubber material combining superior chemical permeation resistance and durability, with smooth soft feel. Also available with silicone facepiece.
Construction Type	Integral nose-cup with controlled air flow; highly elasticized head harness; and facepiece support
Color	Black (blue and yellow available in silicone)

Logistical Parameters

Ease of Use	Lightweight and ergonomically correct facepiece. Highly elasticized head harness with quick-release buckles with rollers for easy donning, simple adjustment and fast removal.
Consumables	Filters
Maintenance Requirements	Not specified
Shelf Life	Not specified
Transportability	Easily transportable
Operational Limitations	Not specified
Environmental Conditions	Normal environments
Unit Cost	Less than $150
Maintenance Cost	Not specified
Warranty	Not specified
Don/Doff Information	Highly elasticized head harness with quick-release buckles with rollers for easy donning, simple adjustment and fast removal
Use/Reuse	Not specified
Launderability	Can be cleaned and reused many times
Accessories	Types of filter canisters available: M80 NBC canister (Israeli Defense Forces NBC filter canister), M38 NBC canister (performance equivalent to U.S. Military C2 NBC canister), A2, A2–P3, A2B2E2–P3, and A2B2E2K2–P3

Special Requirements

Training Requirements	Little training required
Training Available	Not specified
Manuals Available	User manual
Surveillance Testing Requirements	Not specified
Support Equipment	Not applicable
Testing Information	Not specified
Applicable Regulations	Not specified

Health Hazards   Not specified

Communications Interface   Speaking diaphragm for clear voice communication
Capability

EOD Compatibility   Not specified

General

Name
ID# 65

Model 4A1 NBC Respirator (69)

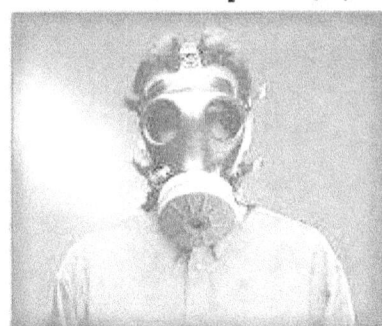

Technology

NBC respirators for civil defense are designed to protect the eyes, face, and respiratory tract of adults and children over the age of 8 yr, from all known NBC agents. Shalon civilian respirators are the standard approved NBC respirators of the Israeli Civil Defense Authorities.

Stock Number

Four models available:
4A1—Adult respirator—one size fits all
10A1—protection of children from age 8 yr and older
Models 4 and 10 are identical to models 4A1 and 10A1 but without voicemitter and drinking system
Panoramic model—single curved impact resistant plastic lense with improved peripheral vision. One size fits all. Designed primarily for industrial and laboratory workers.

Protection Type

Respiratory and percutaneous

Equipment Category

Respirator/single canister type respirator with standard connection

Availability

Commercial

Current User(s)

Civil defense

Manufacturer

Shalon Chemical Industries Ltd.
25, Nahmani St.
Tel-Aviv 65794, Israel
POC: Kenneth Samet, Quality Assurance Manager
972-8-6879111 (Tel)
972-8-6811115 (Fax)

U.S. Distribution:
Sellstrom Manufacturing Co.
Palatine, IL 60067
847-358-2000 (Tel)
847-358-8564 (Fax)

Neoterik Health Tech. Inc.
Woodsboro, MD 21798
301-845-2777 (Tel)
301-845-2213 (Fax)

Manufacturer Type

Foreign

Developer

Shalon Chemical Industries

Source

Internet: www.doryanet.co.il/Shalon/23.htm
www.shalon.co.il
shalon@shalon.co.il

Certification

Not specified

Operational Parameters

Chemical Warfare (CW) Agents Protected Against	All known NBC agents
Biological Warfare (BW) Agents Protected Against	All known NBC agents
Toxic Industrial Materials (TIMs) Protected Against	Not specified
Duration of Protection	Not specified
Recommended Use(s)	Civil defense, laboratory workers, and industrial safety

Physical Parameters

Sizes Available	Adult model 4A1 (one size fits all) Child model 10A1 (ages 8 and older)
Weight	Lightweight and specially designed for extended use with superior comfort, secure fit, and low breathing resistance
Package Size and Volume	Not specified
Power Requirements	Not applicable
Material Type	Specially formulated impermeable rubber material for high resistance to NBC agents. Impact resistant plastic lenses with excellent optics. Elastic head harness.
Construction Type	The adult model incorporates a uniquely designed peripheral sealing lip for a high level of protection for most male and female users
Color	Black

Logistical Parameters

Ease of Use	Five-strap highly elastic head harness for quick easy donning and simple adjustment
Consumables	Filters
Maintenance Requirements	Not specified
Shelf Life	Durable and 20 yr shelf life
Transportability	Easily transportable
Operational Limitations	Drinking system with safety connections for effortless safe drinking in contaminated environments. Comfortable nose cup with controlled air flow to eliminate internal fogging and CO_2 buildup. Low breathing resistance.
Environmental Conditions	Normal environments
Unit Cost	Not specified
Maintenance Cost	Not specified
Warranty	Not specified
Don/Doff Information	Five-strap highly elasticized head harness for easy donning, simple adjustment and fast removal
Use/Reuse	Not specified
Launderability	Can be cleaned and reused many times
Accessories	All models supplied with Shalon's NBC filter canister Type 80, and NATO standard 40 mm threaded canister housing

Special Requirements

Training Requirements	Little training required
Training Available	Not specified
Manuals Available	User manual
Surveillance Testing Requirements	Not specified

Support Equipment	Drinking system with safety connections
Testing Information	Not specified
Applicable Regulations	Not specified
Health Hazards	Not specified
Communications Interface Capability	Voicemitter providing clear effective communication
EOD Compatibility	Not specified

General

Name

ID# 66

M15-A30 NBC Respirator

Technology

Military respirators are the standard official Israel Defense Forces NBC respirator. They are intended for military and police personnel, providing eye, face, and respiratory protection against all known NBC agents. Their design affords optimum comfort and fit, while causing minimal interference with performance of required military drills such as tactical movement, employment of weapons, and effective communication.

Stock Number

Four models available:
M15-A30—economical version of the military respirator (M15-A1T), without a voicemitter or a drinking system (this model has wide applications with the police and civil defense)
M15-A1T—standard official Israeli NBC respirator featuring a side voicemitter for telephone communication
M15-A1—identical to the M15-A1T, but without the side voicemitter
M15-S80—standard Israeli respirator fit tank crews featuring a built-in dynamic microphone and flexible rubber breathing tube

Protection Type

Respiratory and percutaneous

Equipment Category

Respirator/single canister type respirator with standard and military connection

Availability

Commercial

Current User(s)

Military, police, and civil defense

Manufacturer

Shalon Chemical Industries Ltd.
25, Nahmani St.
Tel-Aviv 65794, Israel
POC: Kenneth Samet, Quality Assurance Manager
972–8–6879111 (Tel)
972–8–6811115 (Fax)

U.S. Distribution:
Sellstrom Manufacturing Co.
Palatine, IL 60067
847–358–2000 (Tel)

Manufacturer Type

Foreign

Developer

Shalon Chemical Industries

Source

Internet: www.doryanet.co.il/Shalon/23.htm
www.shalon.co.il
shalon@shalon.co.il

Certification

NIOSH

Operational Parameters

Chemical Warfare (CW) Agents Protected Against

All known NBC agents

Biological Warfare (BW) Agents Protected Against	All known NBC agents
Toxic Industrial Materials (TIMs) Protected Against	All known NBC agents
Duration of Protection	Not specified
Recommended Use(s)	Civil defense, military, police, and industrial safety

Physical Parameters

Sizes Available	All models supplied in 3 sizes (small, medium, and large)
Weight	Lightweight, with a comfortable secure fit and low breathing resistance
Package Size and Volume	Not specified
Power Requirements	Not applicable
Material Type	Specially formulated rubber material for high resistance to NBC agents, superior comfort and durability. Impact resistant cylindrical plastic lenses with wide field of vision. Five-strap highly elastic head harness with quick release buckles.
Construction Type	Three overlapping face-piece sizes assuring reliable fit for over 98 % of mature male and female users. Peripheral sealing lip assuring excellent fit.
Color	Black

Logistical Parameters

Ease of Use	Five-strap highly elastic head harness equipped with quick release buckles for quick easy donning and simple adjustment
Consumables	Filters
Maintenance Requirements	Not specified
Shelf Life	Durable and 20 yr shelf life
Transportability	Easily transportable
Operational Limitations	Drinking system with safety connections for safe drinking in contaminated environments providing extra comfort and extended wear in hot climates and during vigorous drills or exercises. Spectacles mount assemble for prescription eyeglasses. Impact resistant cylindrical plastic lenses with wide field of vision. Low breathing resistance.
Environmental Conditions	Normal environments
Unit Cost	Not specified
Maintenance Cost	Not specified
Warranty	Not specified
Don/Doff Information	Five-strap highly elasticized head harness with quick-release buckles with rollers for easy donning, simple adjustment and fast removal
Use/Reuse	Not specified
Launderability	Can be cleaned and reused many times
Accessories	All models supplied with Shalon's NBC filter canister Type 80, and NATO standard 40 mm threaded canister housing

Special Requirements

Training Requirements	Little training required
Training Available	Not specified
Manuals Available	User manual
Surveillance Testing Requirements	Not specified
Support Equipment	Drinking system with safety connections

Testing Information	Not specified
Applicable Regulations	Not specified
Health Hazards	Not specified
Communications Interface Capability	Dynamic microphone system for communication in tanks and armored vehicles (available only in M15-S80 model)
	Side or central voicemitter for telephone communications
EOD Compatibility	Not specified

General

Name
ID# 67

SE400 Fan Supplied, Positive Pressure Respirator (FPBR)

Technology
The SE400 is a breath responsive, computerized positive pressure PAPR with data logging and positive pressure suit ventilation capability

Stock Number
99-10000
NATO Stock Numbers:
0465-66-147-005—Backpack, fan unit, and air filtering respirator
7030-66-147-0053—Software kit, diagnostics, and respirator air filtering
0405-66-147-0846—Belt, waist, respirator fan unit, and short size
0405-66-147-0047—Belt, waist, respirator fan unit, and long size

Protection Type
Respiratory

Equipment Category
PAPR, positive pressure, and powered respirator

Availability
Commercial

Current User(s)
Special Operation Response Team Inc., SORT, NC
  POC: Walt Caplan 336-759-3924 (Tel)
Office of Emergency Preparedness/National Disaster Medical System, MD
  POC: Bob Cornish 301-443-1307 (Tel)
U.S. Army Soldier and Biological Chemical Command
  POC: Team Leader Frank DiPietro 410-436-2223 (Tel)
City of Indianapolis Department of Public Safety
  POC: Director Stephen Robertson 317-327-3900 (Tel)
City of Pittsburgh Department of Public Safety
  POC: Operations Supervisor Raymond V. DeMichiei 412-255-2293
  (Tel)
Australian Defense Force (Joint Incident Response Unit, JIRU, CBRR Squadron); NSW Police Force (Bomb Investigation and Rorensics); NSW Health Dept. (emergency groups); Mt Isa Mines; Pasminco Mining Group

Manufacturer
SEA Group
11 Business Park Drive
Branford, CT 06405
POC: Bengt Kjellberg, President
203-483-9483 (Tel)
203-483-6633 (Fax)
888-732-3500 (Toll Free U.S. and Canada)
Email :bengtk@sea.com.au
http://www.sea.com.au

Manufacturer Type
Foreign

Developer
SEA Group

Source
Brochure and Internet http://www.sea.com.au

Certification
NIOSH, CE, and Australian work cover

Operational Parameters

Chemical Warfare (CW) Agents Protected Against

Tested and passed GB test

Biological Warfare (BW) Agents Protected Against

Virus and bacterial with P-100 filter. Specification available on request. Call 1–888–732 (ask for document regarding Performance Domestic Preparedness Filter).

Toxic Industrial Materials (TIMs) Protected Against

Acid gases, organic vapors and ammonia, as per NIOSH requirements

Duration of Protection

Meets NIOSH requirements. Batteries will last 4 h to 6 h (heads up display when to change filters)

Recommended Use(s)

In an environment where guaranteed high protection factor, low breathing resistance in combination with long duration time and low weight is needed in combination with data logging and positive pressure suite ventilation

Physical Parameters

Sizes Available

Size options available on facepiece only:
Full face mask: One size available
Half mask: Small, medium, and large

Weight

Complete SE 400 unit 8 lb (including battery and chemical warfare filters)

Package Size and Volume

The SE400 is supplied in 2 cartons. Carton one contains the fan unit and accessories; carton two contains the full-face mask.
Carton one: 20 in x 11 in x 5.5 in
Carton two: 9.4 in x 9.4 in x 7.3 in

Power Requirements

Battery: 12 V dc NiMH rechargeable and custom battery designed for SE400 available from SEA

Material Type

Not applicable

Construction Type

Not applicable

Color

Fan unit: Blue/black
Hose: Black
Full-face mask: Black

Logistical Parameters

Ease of Use

The SE400 can be fitted to a standard SEA waist belt, padded waist belt, or a custom designed backpack. The choice of fittings gives the wearer the greatest flexibility for various working conditions. The SE400 has a single push-button operation. The breath responsive feature is automatic and requires no user intervention. Warning conditions are easily identified by five (5) indicators on the fan unit and a tri-color (red/orange/green) indicator located at the facepiece.

Consumables

Gas and particle filters: domestic preparedness filter—50032; prefilters—27

Maintenance Requirements

The SE400 has a built-in self-test feature and it is recommended, but not essential, that a self-test be performed prior to each shift. The SE400 has built-in diagnostics for checking critical system function and system voltages. If an error is detected, this is recorded in the system log and an alarm sounded to notify the wearer.

Shelf Life

4 °F to 131 °F storage temperature

Transportability

The SE400 can be transported without the need for any special equipment

Operational Limitations

The SE400 is virtually free of breathing resistance therefore there is very little additional workload so the user can perform normal work for longer periods without suffering discomfort

Environmental Conditions

Regulator tested for equivalent 3 yr harsh conditions.
Fan unit: 32 °F to 131 °F operating temperature; 0 % to 90 % relative humidity operation

Unit Cost	Approx $2K for SE 400 complete with 2 rechargeable batteries, harness, test and computer interface cables, speaker box, belt, and software for SE400
Maintenance Cost	No tools
Warranty	3 yr or 6000 h warranty on motor and circuit board. 12 mo on manufacturing defects (not including wear and tear)
Don/Doff Information	There is no assistance required for the donning on or off of the SE400. An experienced operator can comfortably fit the SE400 within 2 min.
Use/Reuse	The only items to be discarded are the consumables (i.e., the filters and prefilters). Disposing of the filters depends on the environment in which they have been used and the type of contaminant they have been filled with.
Launderability	The SE400 can be cleaned using a damp cloth, this information is available in the user manual
Accessories	Mask unit, regulator, fan unit, battery, data log, and computer interface cable

Special Requirements

Training Requirements	No specific training required other than to read the manual. Fifteen (15) min will give the user the basic operational understanding. Further training is required for the user to understand the maintenance and care of the SE400
Training Available	SEA can provide full training for use, maintenance, and care of the SE400. Typical duration is 1 d
Manuals Available	A user manual is supplied with the SE400. Training documentation can be provided.
Surveillance Testing Requirements	The unit features a comprehensive auditing and record-keeping data log that monitors important events
Support Equipment	Sundrom gas and particle filters
Testing Information	Footnotes: 1) Grandjean E. (1988) Fitting the mask to the man, 4th ed, London, pp 83–94. 2) A study of the relation between minute volume and instantaneous peak flows, Sydney 3) Johnson, A.T., et al, Effect of Respirator Inspiratory Level on Constant Load Treadmill Work Performance, Univ. of Maryland, presented at the American Hygienists' Conference, Dallas, TX. 4) Tested by U.S. Army SBCCOM Edgewood Biological and Chemical Center, Aberdeen Proving Ground, MD. Tested and passed GB test. Test parameters available on request 888–732–3500 (Tel). Specification available on request. Call 888–732–3500 and ask for document regarding Performance Domestic Preparedness Filter.
Applicable Regulations	NIOSH, CE
Health Hazards	Not specified
Communications Interface Capability	SE-TALK—a miniature loudspeaker that connects to the respirator unit. It can be clipped to a breast pocket or belt.
EOD Compatibility	

General
Name
ID# 68

Survivair™ Cougar SCBA

Technology

The Survivair Cougar SCBA meets the demands of industrial users who want the finest respiratory protection against environments that are IDLH, but do not require the performance of an NFPA-compliant SCBA

Stock Number

Not specified

Protection Type

Respiratory

Equipment Category

SCBA. The design eliminates unnecessary fire fighting features, keeping costs under control for today's dollar-conscious industrial users, yet providing maximum safety and comfort.

Availability

Commercially

Current User(s)

Not specified

Manufacturer

Survivair
A Division of Bacou USA Safety, Inc.
3001 South Susan Street
Santa Ana, CA 92704

Manufacturer Type

Survivair

Developer

Bullard

Source

www.survivair.com
POC: Lisa Mork APR Product Manager
800-APR-SCBA Tel
714-850-0299 (Fax)
techcomm@deltanet.com
www.survivair.com

Certification

Not specified

Operational Parameters

Chemical Warfare (CW) Agents Protected Against

Not specified

Biological Warfare (BW) Agents Protected Against

Not specified

Toxic Industrial Materials (TIMs) Protected Against

The Survivair Cougar has respiratory protection against environments that are IDLH

Duration of Protection

Not specified

Recommended Use(s)

Not specified

Physical Parameters

Sizes Available
Available in small and standard sizes in blue and black. (Classic™ facepiece).

Weight
One of the lightest, easiest to use, and most comfortable backpacks in the industry

Package Size and Volume
Not specified

Power Requirements
All Survivair PAPRs have powerful motors that provide high airflow rates that exceed the NIOSH requirements for loose and tight fitting headpieces. All PAPRs feature long-lasting battery packs with trouble-free recharging. Battery packs feature a quick-connect power cord and auto-reset fuse, and a rated 8 h life to last a full work shift.

Material Type
Silicone rubber, five-strap head harness and skirt, optional Headnet™, easily removable exhalation valve, better sealing ability for improved comfort and fit. Mesh style head harness for those who prefer this style.

Construction Type
One of the lightest, easiest-to-use, and most comfortable backpacks in the industry. No bolts or screws on harness for quick, easy disassembly and assembly. Conveniently holds regulator in activated stand-by position. Keeps contaminants and water out of disconnected regulator.

Color
Available in three color-coded sizes. (TwentyTwenty® facepiece).

Logistical Parameters

Ease of Use
Compact, low profile Air Klic™ fastening system First-Breath-On. Better downward vision, less chance of damage. Allows attachment in any orientation. Activation of unit without free flow. Can be kept in stand-by mode.

Consumables
Not specified

Maintenance Requirements
Fast and easy servicing

Shelf Life
Not specified

Transportability
Not specified

Operational Limitations
Unsurpassed comfort and even in extreme heat or cold

Environmental Conditions
Durable. Will not oxidize or react with ozone.

Unit Cost
Not specified

Maintenance Cost
First stage regulator. Minimal moving parts dramatically enhances reliability, while reducing maintenance costs

Warranty
Not specified

Don/Doff Information
Not specified

Use/Reuse
Not specified

Launderability
Not specified

Accessories
Backpack

Special Requirements

Training Requirements
Not specified

Training Available
Not specified

Manuals Available
Not specified

Surveillance Testing Requirements
Not specified

Support Equipment
Gauge and alarm assembly

Testing Information
Not specified

Applicable Regulations
Not specified

Health Hazards	Not specified
Communications Interface Capability	Not specified
EOD Compatibility	Not specified

General

Name
ID# 69

Survivair™ Belt Mounted PAPR

Technology

PAPR; Maximum airflow, and hassle free operation.
All Survivair PAPRs have powerful motors that provide high airflow rates, which exceed the NIOSH requirements for loose and tight fitting headpieces. All PAPRs feature long-lasting battery packs with trouble-free recharging. Battery packs feature a quick-connect power cord and auto-reset fuse, and a rated 8 h life to last a full work shift.

Stock Number
Name from ERDEC-TR

Protection Type
Respiratory

Equipment Category
PAPR, maximum air flow, with motors, and recharging battery pack

Availability
Commercially

Current User(s)
Not specified

Manufacturer
Survivair
A Division of Bacou USA Safety, Inc.
3001 South Susan Street
Santa Ana, CA 92704

Manufacturer Type
Survivair

Developer
Bullard

Source
www.survivair.com
POC: Lisa Mork APR Product Manager
800-APR-SCBA Tel
714-850-0299 (Fax)
techcomm@deltanet.com
www.survivair.com

Certification
NIOSH Approval No. TC-23C-1053; Intrinsically Safe. All PAPRs have been tested and listed by SGS U.S. Testing Company, Inc., as meeting the ANSI/UL 913 standard for intrinsically safe apparatus for use in Class 1, Division 1, Groups A, B, C, and D hazardous locations.

Operational Parameters

Chemical Warfare (CW) Agents Protected Against
Not specified

Biological Warfare (BW) Agents Protected Against
Not specified

Toxic Industrial Materials (TIMs) Protected Against
Not specified

Duration of Protection
Not specified

Recommended Use(s)
Not specified

Physical Parameters

Sizes Available   Small and standard sizes

Weight   Survivair's mask mounted PAPR weighs only 59 ounces. The belt mounted units weigh a bit more.

Package Size and Volume   Not specified

Power Requirements   All Survivair PAPRs have powerful motors that provide high air flow rates, which exceed the NIOSH requirements for loose and tight fitting headpieces. All PAPRs feature long-lasting battery packs with trouble-free recharging. Battery packs feature a quick-connect power cord and auto-reset fuse, and a rated 8 h life to last a full work shift.

Material Type   Choice of silicone full facepiece, silicone half mask, or Tyvek® single bib hood

Construction Type   Not specified

Color   Not specified

Logistical Parameters

Ease of Use   Single bib hood covers neck and collar area, providing splash/overspray/ skin absorption protection and easy wearer cleanup. Single bib hood fits persons with facial hair or prescription glasses; the only alternative to tight-fitting facepieces. Single bib hood easily accommodates a hard hat when head protection is required. Belt mounted battery pack and blower/filter assembly are designed to ride comfortably on the wearer's hip, thus taking the weight off the facepiece.

Consumables   Not specified

Maintenance Requirements   Not specified

Shelf Life   Not specified

Transportability   Not specified

Operational Limitations   Not specified

Environmental Conditions   Not specified

Unit Cost   Not specified

Maintenance Cost   Not specified

Warranty   Not specified

Don/Doff Information   Not specified

Use/Reuse   Not specified

Launderability   Not specified

Accessories   All full facepieces come standard with a speaking diaphragm to enhance wearer communication. Optional 5 unit and 10 unit chargers available as accessories.

Special Requirements

Training Requirements   Not specified

Training Available   Not specified

Manuals Available   Not specified

Surveillance Testing Requirements   Not specified

Support Equipment   Not specified

Testing Information   Not specified

Applicable Regulations   Not specified

Health Hazards   Not specified

Communications Interface   All full facepieces come standard with a speaking diaphragm to enhance
Capability   wearer communication
EOD Compatibility   Not specified

ABOUT THE LAW ENFORCEMENT AND CORRECTIONS STANDARDS AND TESTING PROGRAM

The Law Enforcement and Corrections Standards and Testing Program is sponsored by the Office of Science and Technology of the National Institute of Justice (NIJ), U.S. Department of Justice. The program responds to the mandate of the Justice System Improvement Act of 1979, directed NIJ to encourage research and development to improve the criminal justice system and to disseminate the results to Federal, State, and local agencies.

The Law Enforcement and Corrections Standards and Testing Program is an applied research effort that determines the technological needs of justice system agencies, sets minimum performance standards for specific devices, tests commercially available equipment against those standards, and disseminates the standards and the test results to criminal justice agencies nationally and internationally.

The program operates through:

The *Law Enforcement and Corrections Technology Advisory Council* (LECTAC), consisting of nationally recognized criminal justice practitioners from Federal, State, and local agencies, which assesses technological needs and sets priorities for research programs and items to be evaluated and tested.

The *Office of Law Enforcement Standards* (OLES) at the National Institute of Standards and Technology, which develops voluntary national performance standards for compliance testing to ensure that individual items of equipment are suitable for use by criminal justice agencies. The standards are based upon laboratory testing and evaluation of representative samples of each item of equipment to determine the key attributes, develop test methods, and establish minimum performance requirements for each essential attribute. In addition to the highly technical standards, OLES also produces technical reports and user guidelines that explain in nontechnical terms the capabilities of available equipment.

The *National Law Enforcement and Corrections Technology Center* (NLECTC), operated by a grantee, which supervises a national compliance testing program conducted by independent laboratories. The standards developed by OLES serve as performance benchmarks against which commercial equipment is measured. The facilities, personnel, and testing capabilities of the independent laboratories are evaluated by OLES prior to testing each item of equipment, and OLES helps the NLECTC staff review and analyze data. Test results are published in Equipment Performance Reports designed to help justice system procurement officials make informed purchasing decisions.

Publications are available at no charge through the National Law Enforcement and Corrections Technology Center. Some documents are also available online through the Internet/World Wide Web. To request a document or additional information, call 800–248–2742 or 301–519–5060, or write:

National Law Enforcement and Corrections Technology Center
P.O. Box 1160
Rockville, MD 20849–1160
E-Mail: *asknlectc@nlectc.org*
World Wide Web address: *http://www.nlectc.org*

The National Institute of Justice is a component of the Office of Justice Programs, which also includes the Bureau of Justice Assistance, the Bureau of Justice Statistics, the Office of Juvenile Justice and Delinquency Prevention, and the Office for Victims of Crime.